"Have you ever wondered whether you [...] lowing someone else's directions? Roni Ku [...] [...] guide to finding your keys to self-discovery, filled with easy exercises and notes on keeping a personal journal. She will inspire you to create your own charmed life!"

—Chellie Campbell, Author of *The Wealthy Spirit* and *From Worry to Wealthy*

"Roni Kugler's *12 Ways to Discover What Makes You Tick* is a soul-searching journey launched by her own experiences and insights. The investment of your time and energy—with Roni's guidance—can generate new directions with your own struggles, providing hope and possibilities for the changes you are seeking. Knowing what makes you tick is the critical platform upon which to build your future."

—Paul J. Friday, Ph.D., Author of *Friday's Law*

"As a therapist, what I love about this book is that it actually makes approaching our problems in life easy, fun, and nonthreatening. At the end of it, you really know yourself and what makes you tick. This is a great book."

—Dr. Helena Cerney, Ph.D., MFT

"I love this book because it does exactly what it says. Whether looking at divorce, single parenting, abuse, or starting over, *12 Ways to Discover What Makes You Tick* provides a unique, refreshing, ACTUALLY fun way of transforming challenges into amazing opportunities for the best outcome."

—Steve Soldinger, Board Certified Psychiatrist, MD, President of the Southern California Psychiatric Society 2013–2014

Enjoy the read!
Roni

12 WAYS TO DISCOVER WHAT MAKES YOU TICK

RONI L. KUGLER

Email: Roni12Ways@gmail.com

Website: www.Ronikugler.com

ISBN: 978-0-692-71930-5

"You are who you are because of or despite your upbringing."

—Sidney Stern, my father

This book is dedicated to my family.

Table of Contents

Preface

"For the past several years many people have been talking about the passing of Steve Jobs and how his innovations have changed the world. From the iPod to the iPad to the iPhone, his products have changed the way we communicate and see ourselves. Well, I have been fortunate to have the only iFriend, Roni. She has changed the way I communicate and see myself and others. Her passion for life and her ability to share herself has made her an inspiration to others. Roni is a dedicated, exemplary friend! She keeps believing in you when you have ceased to believe in yourself."

—A dear friend

I have been told my whole life that I tend to get to the heart of a problem without judgment. I have been complimented by those I come in contact with, as they say that after talking with me they feel hopeful, they see possibilities, and they feel better about themselves.

This has been my motivation to write my story and the lessons I have learned. I hope that what I have to share brings you value and helps you to live a life of passion and joy.

—Roni Kugler

Introduction

Each chapter in this book begins with a story from my life and serves as a springboard for you as the reader to think about your own life. I then give examples of what I did to work through my various challenges. I talk about what worked for me and what didn't work. At this point I provide exercises that you can use to learn more about your own situation. Because we all learn differently, I also list suggestions so that you can find the exercise that works best for you.

I recommend that you use a journal or an electronic device to keep track of your progress so you can always be aware of how you are feeling and doing regarding the subjects discussed in this book.

Listen to Your Inner Voice

I grew up in a household like many others, with parents who knew very little about raising children. My dad was a pilot in World War II. My mother was a housewife who stayed at home to raise us three kids. My father's parenting tactics were pretty much formed from his experiences in the military. He was taught to take orders and not question authority. There was an expectation of keeping one's feelings hidden.

It also didn't help that my grandmother, whom I loved dearly, was bossy, controlling, and opinionated. My dad seemed to inherit these traits. He expected all of us, including my mother, to be compliant and obedient. What he told us was that if he didn't control our behavior, he thought we would not be capable of making what he considered proper decisions.

We were never given an explanation when we questioned why he wanted us to do something he considered important. His mantra was, "Because I say so." Even when we were older, he imposed his opinions and will on us. His philosophy was, "My way or the highway."

My mother's job was to please my father, which included backing him up, even when she did not agree with how he parented us. She told me when I was a teenager that she would have done things differently if my father had not been such a strong-willed person and she had not felt so powerless.

I was the only girl. My older brother was born three years before me, and my younger brother followed me by four. As the typical middle child, I was the negotiator and was always fighting to find my place within the family. It didn't help that my older brother excelled at everything he did. I frequently felt inferior and that I would be a disappointment to my parents. Whether it was in school, on the playground, or at the piano, everything seemed to come easy to him. I started out trying to please my parents, but never felt that I could. It was a cross that I would bear for most of my life.

Because I never seemed to measure up to my brother's performance, I relied on my personality and didn't make much of an effort in school, even though I had been told that I was bright.

All of the pressures of childhood caused me to underachieve. If something was not easy, I simply didn't try.

At a very early age, as young as five, I started to have conversations with myself. When something didn't feel right to me, I was able to comfort myself. I used my imagination to create a life that made me feel safe.

At the time, I wasn't aware of what this process was called. I now know this was my inner voice. This helped me to learn ways to protect myself.

I learned at a very early age to keep my feelings inside, mostly because my dad was uncomfortable with our expressing emotions, specifically anger and tears.

I also developed the skill of defending and being defensive. This was a survival tool that I held on to for many decades. Basically, I learned to duck and/or stay out of the way. We weren't physically hit; however, we were verbally abused. My dad called me stupid, knucklehead, and knothead. In my twenties, I was convinced that my headaches were due to years of believing that there was something wrong with my head. My mother didn't like rocking the boat, and although she was involved in our lives, she took a very passive role in raising us.

I didn't always know what was right for me; however, I always knew what didn't feel right. I spent many years, actually decades, trying to figure out why I made certain decisions. I think I was trying to understand what made me tick long before I even knew what that meant.

I realize now that there were countless times that my inner voice was guiding me in ways that I couldn't understand at the time.

After high school I enrolled at a local junior college. I was interested in journalism and acting classes. It was at this time that I met the guy I was to marry. Although he was really nice and I truly thought I was in love, the reality was that I married to get out of the house. I was 19 years old. With the entire family already planning to attend my wedding, I knew I made a mistake. I was more nervous than I thought I should be. I was having trouble sleeping. I was picturing a life with him, and it just didn't feel right. Once again, there was my inner voice, loud and clear.

The night before we were to be married, I called him on the phone and spent about 15 minutes telling him all the reasons why I didn't think we should go through with this. He assured me that I was having normal pre-wedding jitters and that everything was going to be fine. I DID NOT listen to my inner voice. I overrode what I knew was probably a bad idea in order to escape an unhappy childhood. It didn't occur to me that at 19 I could go out on my own. In 1969 there seemed to be fewer options and choices for women. Taking off for New York was a dream of mine, but I was too young and immature to take chances. And I couldn't rely on my family to encourage me to follow my dreams.

Not only did I marry way too young, but I also quit college after just two years to get a job in order to support my husband while he went to school. This was to become a pattern of putting off my needs to support my partners.

We were married less than five years. Although the marriage didn't last, I will never have regrets, because my beautiful son Ryan was born from it.

Even though many of you might be familiar with your personal inner voice, not everyone is. And for each of us, it can be different. For some people, it is a very clear voice that lets us know if something doesn't feel right. Or it lets us know if we are going in the right direction.

For others, it's not that clear. Our heart may race a bit or we may feel uncomfortable. We might have a hard time swallowing or our stomach may feel queasy. Our fingers could feel tingly. It can even be as subtle as doubt sneaking into our thoughts.

Like me, are you marrying for the wrong reasons? Or are you making a career choice that doesn't suit you? It can even be as small a decision as being talked into a vacation destination you don't want to go to, or it could be buying an expensive car that you can't afford. If I can give you one thing to walk away with here, it would be that "ignoring your inner voice is NOT in your best interest."

Throughout the rest of this chapter, there are exercises that you might find useful in helping you to become aware of what your inner voice feels like. I'd like to encourage you to get a journal or pad of paper to use exclusively for your thoughts and exercises that I provide in this book. It is very important that you begin journaling your responses, not just thinking about your answers. It has been proven, regardless of the subject, that writing tends to help you pay attention to what is going on. Journaling also gives you the ability to review what you've discovered about yourself and/or add more information as your new thoughts come and go throughout the day.

1. Take a week or two to become aware of your decision-making process. This includes, but is not limited to, really paying attention when it comes time to make a decision. This could be at work, with your spouse, with your kids, with your parents, etc. Pay close attention to how you *feel* about your decisions. Do you feel that it is a 100 percent correct decision, or are you questioning yourself? What happens after you've made your decision? Are you at peace with it; can you let it go? Do you have a nagging worry or doubt? These are all examples of what an inner voice is, and these are all examples of what you should be writing down.

    Pay careful attention to *your* signs. Do you feel as if someone is whispering in your ear? Do you sense something that doesn't quite feel comfortable? Does your heart race a bit, or does your stomach feel unsettled? The butterflies in your stomach tell you something. Your uneasiness tells you something. You can benefit by being more in tune with your mind and body. This will help you to identify the fears and anxieties that are holding you back or causing you concern. Again, write down your thoughts and feelings.

2. What I would like you to do now is to think about a time when you *didn't* listen to your inner voice. Make a list of these instances.

3. Now take whatever time you need to think about the consequences of not listening to your inner voice. For me, it was marrying for the wrong reasons. Get in touch with how you were affected, and start writing this down. Whether you write key words or full sentences, what's important is that you are starting to pay attention to you. List everything that comes to your mind, even if you don't see the importance.

   Around the time I turned twenty, I remember reading an article regarding anger. The advice was to NOT express yourself right at the moment you felt like exploding. It went on to explain that by simply taking the time to count to ten, your heart rate would slow down, thus allowing you to become calmer before you talked. Instead of coming from a place of rage, which you could later regret, there would be a better chance that conversations would be more rational. I decided to use this simple method to do just that before making any decisions. This allowed me the time to really pay attention not just to what my head was telling me, but also to my body.

   Whether I made a decision to change jobs, go out on a date, make a large purchase, or move, I started a lifetime practice of paying attention to how I was feeling, what my body was telling me. In other words, I was beginning to recognize and pay attention to my inner voice.

I remember a time in my mid-thirties when I was torn between staying at a job that was secure yet unsatisfying, or taking a risk on a new company with potential to really grow and learn. To say my mind was divided is an understatement. Although my ex-husband was very involved in my son's life, I wasn't receiving much child support. My child's needs were at the top of the list of all the decisions I made. I spent more than a week weighing the pros and cons of taking this new job. I obsessed about all the positives and negatives. In general I was making myself nuts.

One evening right before I needed to make my decision, I sat on the stairs in front of my house. The night was clear and quiet. I remember saying out loud to no one in particular, "Help. I just don't know what to do." It was at that moment that I decided to simply pay attention to my body as I pictured myself making the choice to stay, and then pictured myself making the choice to move on. I looked at worst- and best-case scenarios. Then I cleared my mind and I went to sleep.

After a good night's sleep, to my amazement, I had clarity. I made the decision to take the risk. As soon as I decided to move on, I felt less stressed and anxious. I then began a journey that turned out to be the first step in my career taking a positive upward turn. In this instance, I listened to my inner voice, which guided me to go down this path.

4. Take some time to make a list of the times that you did listen to your inner voice. Write these down. Consider all the struggles you were dealing with. It could be small ones or ones that had a bigger impact on your life.

5. After you read over your list, think about what the consequences were of listening to your inner voice. Were you more comfortable with the choices you made? Did you feel that you paid more attention to your

body? Were your processes different than mine? There is no right or wrong way to do this. It is, after all, your journey. Now make your list of these consequences. Sometimes just seeing things in print gives you perspective.

It is so important for all of us to understand why we make the decisions we do. It is essential to pay close attention to our decision-making processes. This way we learn from our mistakes. In fact, most successful people will say that they learned more from their failures than their successes. No matter what our choices are, we should be using our experiences as a gauge for future decisions. We build upon what we have learned, whether the outcome is positive or negative. There is ALWAYS something of value, if we will just pay attention.

The key to understanding how you tick is to get in tune with your inner voice. Look at it as a conscious awareness that is uniquely yours, and a true gift.

6. When you find yourself struggling to hear your inner voice, find a place that is quiet, one where you can be with your thoughts and feelings. Turn off the TV and put your mobile phone on vibrate or silence. This will assist you in paying attention to what your mind is telling you. This, in turn, will help you to become more aware of what your body is feeling. I believe we could all use time in which we're truly alone. We are so attached to our electronic devices and outside noise that it is almost impossible to be in tune with our thoughts.

Understanding and listening to your physical reactions can be very empowering. The body tells us when things feel right or not. Don't ignore these signs. By paying attention, it should be easier for you to determine whether the decisions you make are in your best interest.

If you still have challenges in being in tune with your inner voice or finding the time to do this, I suggest the following:

7. While doing "mindless" chores such as ironing, washing dishes, tending your garden, etc., let your mind relax and picture some of the situations you have faced, or are currently facing, and how you feel about them. Perhaps while you are in the car waiting to pick up your kids, think about the decisions that still need to be made. It isn't important where you find the space and time to learn to pay attention to your mind and body; it is, however, important that you do it. By keeping your journal with you, when you become aware of something significant, you can jot it down. For those who tend to use their electronic devices, they are wonderful for recording thoughts.

In summary, I strongly suggest following this plan. Find time every day to be with yourself. Allow your thoughts to be whatever they are. Use whatever senses you feel will aid you in truly paying attention to your particular signs—the ones that help you to understand your own body. These could be visual or auditory. Become aware of your body. How does it feel? Calm? Serene? Or do you feel nervous? Perhaps uncomfortable? Pay attention to your internal dialogue. What are your body and mind trying to tell you? Each day, write down your thoughts and feelings. Remember, there are no right or wrong answers. What you want to accomplish here is to spend quiet time and think about where your thoughts go. Get to know yourself in a way you haven't before.

Don't underestimate how important your inner voice is. Think of it as the core of who you are and the first real step in understanding how you tick.

Standing Up for Yourself

I knew his touching me was wrong. The knots I felt in my stomach confirmed it, as I always felt as if I was going to throw up when I thought of him. I can remember my mother talking on the phone with her friends about how much I had changed. She said I went from being a happy kid to one who was sullen and quiet. She even started to get angry with me because I was becoming very moody. I believe she chalked it up to my becoming a teenager.

I grew up in an area that could be compared to Mayberry. Pressed up against the Verdugo Mountains, Sunland was isolated from the San Fernando Valley, and unless I took a bus to the Montrose/Glendale area (which I couldn't do until I was 13), my entire world ranged from the local park to the bowling alley. From one end of the town to the other was about three miles.

We had four elementary schools, one junior high school, and one high school. Those of us who lived in this area knew most of the same kids from the time we were five until we graduated from high school and left home.

This made it all the more difficult for me, as it was extremely hard to avoid him.

My dad worked nights and slept during the day. My mom didn't drive and was the typical fifties housewife. Her life and activities were spent in three square blocks. A large part of her job was to keep the house quiet so my dad could sleep. My brothers and I were rambunctious and she was always nervous we'd wake up our dad. As soon as we got back from school, we grabbed a snack, got on our bikes, and took off. Sometimes to the park, sometimes to the corner ice cream

13

shop, or sometimes to hang with a friend in an alley. Most of the time we didn't return home until the sun started to go down. Life in the fifties and sixties was very different than it is today.

It was an innocent time, a time when most people didn't lock the doors on their houses, and they kept the keys in their unlocked cars.

I knew that if I told my parents what was going on, they would blame me. Or, at least, that is what I thought. I was becoming increasingly uncomfortable with myself and what we were doing. I felt ashamed. He was several years older than me. He was bigger and stronger, and he pressured me whenever I saw him. I felt powerless.

I tried to isolate myself. I changed my habits and patterns to avoid him. Without explaining why I was acting odd, this was very difficult. I really didn't know what to do or who to trust. Although talking with an adult figure would have been helpful, my lack of trust got in my way. Again, I thought I would be blamed.

During this time, focusing in school became an issue. My teachers told my parents that I was not concentrating in class. They were also told that I was acting out, and therefore I spent a lot of time sitting on the stairs outside of class. To say that I was angry and frustrated much of the time would be an understatement.

I spent the nighttime thinking about what was going on, which caused me to have sleepless nights and tiring days. Most of my time was spent in a constant state of nervousness. At a time when I should have been looking forward to meeting boys and dating, I became fearful and isolated, and concerned that I would be taken advantage of.

Eventually it got to a point where I knew I had to do something. It became clear to me that I needed to confide in someone. I had one friend in the neighborhood who was a couple of years older than me. I decided to take a chance and tell her what was going on. I was looking for her to advise me to talk with an adult. Looking for her to tell me what a horrible thing this young man was doing. Looking for her to tell me this wasn't my fault.

Every Saturday I would go by her house and we would walk to the park. One day, while walking, and not facing her, I simply said, "I have a secret." She asked me what it was, and I told her that a boy in the neighborhood was touching me. I waited for her to say something. I was shocked when she finally started to talk. She said that she also had been sexually abused. She told me her brother was her abuser. Instead of her being horrified and in shock, instead of her telling me how wrong the boy was, she told me that this is what young girls should expect and that we had to put up with it.

After that talk, our friendship ended. We had a hard time even looking at each other. We shared a secret, and instead of leaning on each other for comfort and help, this caused us both to be distant. She was one of my only friends in the neighborhood, and I now found myself also avoiding her.

I continued to keep to myself and not share my feelings. Externally, I tried to appear happy and carefree to my friends. Internally, I felt very much alone and as if no one would ever understand me.

To say I was confused, disappointed, and alone is yet another understatement. I knew *it* was wrong. I knew *it* needed to stop. I also knew that although I had expressed my feelings to him over and over again, and although I had cried and told him to leave me alone, it wasn't enough.

There finally came a time when I just couldn't take it anymore. I knew that I needed to speak up for myself in a way he would understand. I knew that I should come from a place of strength, courage, and outrage.

I knew that nothing could be worse than what I was going through. I started by practicing in front of the mirror in my bedroom. I practiced angry faces and made my voice sound stronger than I felt it was.

I picked the day I would talk with him. I remember it so clearly. I met him in the park and told him to stop or I would tell my parents. Although I had told him to stop before, this time it was different. I felt stronger and expressed my feelings loudly and clearly, and with a lot of anger. I had finally become less concerned about the consequences of my parents knowing and more concerned about what I was being subjected to.

As a result, he knew that I would go through with my threat. I was both surprised and relieved when he actually backed away. The more I spoke my mind, the more I felt in control of myself, the weaker he became. I *wasn't* a victim any longer.

Has there been a time in your life, or many times, when you didn't stand up for yourself? Are you facing this now? Your experiences might not be as extreme as mine, although they may be. For you, it could be that you were at the market with a few items to buy and the person in front of you had an entire basket. You were in a hurry, but you never asked this person if you could go first. We can all relate to sitting in a doctor's office waiting for our appointment. Rather than going up to the receptionist and mentioning how long you had been sitting, you stayed quiet and waited—even if it meant you were going to be late for another appointment.

Or, it could be even more serious, such as being in school when you witnessed someone being bullied, or perhaps you were the target of someone else's bullying. It doesn't matter if the subject is being abused by a partner, being unfairly treated by your boss, or having your children talk back to you. Do you take the abuse? Or do you stand up for yourself?

1. Make a list of the people in your life that you have had or continue to have a hard time standing up to. Remember to use your journal, notebook, or electronic device.

2. Now write down the specific situations when you did not stand up for yourself.

3. Think about how this made you feel. What emotions were you experiencing? It isn't important whether you write key words or full sentences. What is important is that you take the time to get in touch with those instances and your emotions, and that you write down how you felt. Be honest with yourself; these exercises are for your eyes only. Unless you want to share it with someone, no one but you will read this.

   I was running for class secretary when I was 13. I remember my dad asking if I was going to vote for myself. I did not plan to vote for myself. I thought if I did, I would be considered conceited or better than the other candidates. Although this was a closed election, I still wasn't comfortable putting the check by my name.

   I shared my thoughts with my dad. He simply said, "Why would someone else vote for you if you don't even have the confidence that you are good enough for the job?" This ended up being a time when I did stand up for myself. I actually started campaigning, voted for myself, and I won the election.

   Believing in ourselves is one of the first and most important steps in getting what we want. Once we start speaking up and standing up for ourselves, we gain confidence and start to feel we have something worthwhile and positive to offer. It is then that others will begin to look to us for our opinions and leadership. We live in a competitive world. It's not about knocking someone else down to get what we want; it is, however, about building ourselves up to attain our goals and dreams. Empowerment comes from believing our own voice has value. Inner strength comes from standing up for yourself.

4. Now think about the times when you *did* stand up for yourself. Write down these circumstances.

5. Additionally, think about how it made you feel to speak up for yourself. What were your emotions? How were you standing? For instance, were you standing straight and tall or were you slumped over? Was your voice confident or was it soft and quivering? Did you feel empowered or did you feel apologetic for expressing yourself?

    If it is difficult for you to stand up for yourself, try the following exercises:

6. Go back to your list where you wrote down the people that you have a hard time standing up to. Your mother-in-law? Your child's teacher? Your next-door neighbor? Or is it pretty much everyone? List these people again.

7. Next to each name, write down what you would really like to say to them. As an option, take out your recorder or use your mobile phone to record yourself. Then play it back and listen to how you sound. Get used to hearing your own voice while you express your thoughts, feelings, and opinions. Try standing in front of a mirror and looking at your body language while you are speaking. Do you look uncomfortable? Are you uncomfortable? How is your eye contact? Are you looking at the person you are talking to or are you looking down? The best person to evaluate you is you. Find a time and place where you can be alone to do this exercise. Talk out loud and critique yourself. This may seem silly at first, but after a while, you will realize that you know yourself better than anyone in your life. Learn to value your voice.

8. Take a week or two to notice all the times and circumstances in which you want to stand up for yourself and don't. Note your feelings of inadequacy that come up. It can be as simple as telling your children they can't go somewhere or do something. It might be telling friends that you are too tired or don't feel like going out. Pay attention to every circumstance. Try to push through the discomfort and begin standing up or speaking up for yourself.

   The point of these exercises is for you to become comfortable and confident speaking your mind. Whether you are learning a new language, starting a new sport, or learning to play an instrument, practice is the key to success.

   We all know that when certain people speak, others listen. What is it that they have? Why do some people command a room and others shrink into the background? I believe it is very simple. Those people are comfortable with who they are.

9. It is time to make a list of those people whom you admire, the ones who speak their minds and stand up for themselves.

   Did you list yourself? If not, why not? Why don't you feel as if your opinions and thoughts are as important as someone else's?

   Please keep in mind that the point of these exercises is to give you self-confidence; they are not meant to be used to overpower or bully someone else.

   Isn't it time you started speaking up and/or standing up for yourself?

Honor Yourself

After high school I attended a local junior college. I wanted to study theater and take creative writing classes. Acting and writing were the only two things that interested me as far as a career choice was concerned. I couldn't see myself doing anything else.

From the time I entered junior high school until my mid-forties, my secret dream was to be on stage. I tried out for every school production in junior high and was told I was a natural. I found it easy to express my emotions by pretending to be someone else. While in my real world crying and anger were suppressed, on the stage I was an open book.

My teachers told my parents that they should help me to pursue the arts. My English teachers gave me high praises on my creative writing. I was encouraged to keep a diary and write stories.

Although I had my dreams, my folks talked about my becoming a secretary or a teacher. That's what girls were encouraged to do in the mid-sixties. That or get married, have children, and be a stay-at-home mother while your husband supported you.

Despite my parents' objections, I entered junior college as a theater arts major. There was a time when I would have listened to them. However, this was so important to me that I stood my ground. And for the first time in many years I looked forward to going to school and being part of creating an imaginary world. A world I loved. I chose to take creative writing classes to fill my English requirements and found myself in a world of possibilities and fantasies.

I was so happy that on my off days I volunteered to help build the sets that we used for the productions.

While school was wonderful, home life was not. My dad did not seem to mellow with age. And my mother seemed to fade even more into the background.

My older brother got married and moved out around this time. He was 21 and I was 18. He had been the number-one person my dad battled with, and without his presence, it was my turn. My younger brother was 14 and was pretty much left alone. He was very sweet, and still is to this day.

I was frustrated and becoming increasingly moody, as it seemed as if every conversation with my parents became a battle of wits. I remember one particularly horrible evening when I started crying to my mother about my dad's constant badgering and bullying. Her response to my being so upset was that with my brother gone, it was now my turn, and I was going to have to learn to deal with my father's bullying ways.

She gave me a lame reason like, "Accept what you can't change."

The year after I started college, I met a guy at a dance who was to become my husband. He was studying to be an accountant and had a couple of years left before he was to graduate. After a year of dating, we got engaged. I quit the theater department and started taking secretarial classes so that I could find work to support us while he finished school, therefore putting my dreams on hold. Looking back now, I realize what a mistake that was. I was starting a lifetime pattern of putting aside what I wanted to please someone else. I wasn't honoring me.

After a couple of years of marriage that were rocky at best, we decided to have a child. It was one of the few things we both agreed on, and the best thing we ever did. I couldn't have asked for a better father for my son. Although he and I looked good on paper, in reality we were very different people who wanted very different things out of life.

It's really hard to know the exact moment when a person realizes they aren't living their own life. We all start out trying to please our parents. Then our friends. After that, our spouses and children, if we have any. We go on to please our bosses, our co-workers, and on and on it goes. It amazes me that we are called the "me" generation, and yet when it comes to the really important things, we try to please everyone *except* ourselves.

Have you ever thought about what it means to honor yourself? If I were to ask you if you knew what honoring your parents and/or grandparents meant, would that be easier for you to answer? To me, words like "respect" and "value" come to mind. Are you treating yourself with the same level of care that you give to those you love?

1. Open your journal and write down what you think honoring yourself means.

2. Take a few minutes to look over your list. After reading it over, write down how much of this list you actually do. This is a time for honesty. Are you truly doing these things for yourself?

3. If you aren't practicing your list, why aren't you? Or if you are drawing a blank and can't even make a list, why can't you? What do you think prevents you from honoring yourself? Write down your feelings now.

    Some people feel they don't deserve to be taken care of. Some people feel they don't deserve to take care of themselves. Others think it is self-indulgent; they don't believe they are worthy. For others it could be messages they received growing up. It could be messages we give to ourselves.

4. Think hard about what you were taught as a child. Spend some time reflecting on what messages you got from family and friends. What did

you tell yourself? These could be words you said to yourself or subtle messages you received. Take the time now to write these down.

5. Would you judge someone else if they told you they did things to honor themselves? Or would you think that is great? Take a few minutes to write down some of your thoughts.

  The point of these exercises is that when you go over your notes later, you might find the perspective you could be missing. You might start to understand why it is so difficult for you to honor or respect yourself.

6. There are definite benefits to honoring yourself. Can you list some? Do you know why honoring yourself is so important? Do you really think it makes a difference?

  Think about these questions. Instead of quickly writing your answers, take the time to think about how you really feel. Take a moment to close your eyes and picture times when you might have felt you weren't good enough. Think about your parents. Did your mom ever take time for herself? Was your dad always working? Did you buy into "A woman's job is never done"? Or, "Keep your nose to the grindstone"? Although these expressions might seem old (and they are), or silly (and they are), some of us store the information and act on it without realizing it. It could be years later that we don't understand why we feel guilty when we take a day off work to just kick back. Or why we give our friends or ourselves excuses if we just hang out playing video games, watching TV, or reading a book.

  Somewhere we were told that unless we are productive, we are lazy. Somewhere the message was given to us that having time to ourselves is self-indulgent.

My opinion is, yes, it is extremely important, and yes, it makes a huge difference to honor, respect, and take care of ourselves.

Have you ever thought about why we are instructed to put on our safety mask before we put one on our children during an emergency while flying? Have you ever heard the expression, "I'm taking care of number one"? Have you ever thought about why these are both so important?

7. Until you start taking care of yourself, it is virtually impossible to care for someone else. Self-respect comes before respect for others. This might seem like a hard concept to grasp for some. You really need to think about what it means to *you*. Take the time to jot down your feelings about what you just read.

8. Ask yourself the following questions, then write down your answers.

   A. Can you really handle your tired children if you are tired yourself?
   B. Can you really offer strength to a friend in need if you don't feel strong yourself?
   C. Can you really be there emotionally for a family member if you're emotionally depleted?

9. Take some time now to make a list of what your dreams are for yourself.

   A. What are the things you wanted to accomplish in the past?
   B. What are the things you would like to accomplish now?

   What is important to you? Not what you think you should be doing. What would you like to do? Take up a new language? Learn how to change the tires on your car? Feel more comfortable patching a hole in the wall (one of my personal goals)? Volunteer at a local shelter or home for the aged? Go back to school to finish your degree? Whether it is a big undertaking or a small one, it doesn't really matter. What matters is that this is your life, and if there are things that you would like to do, what holds you back?

Again, keep in mind that not everything on your list needs to be life-changing. It can be as simple as getting into shape. It could be trying new recipes for your family. Or it could be finishing a project you started, or getting involved in your community. It can be as challenging as changing careers or moving to a new city. Or perhaps calling friends that you've lost touch with.

No matter what your age and no matter what you have done or have yet to do, remember that it is *never* too late to realize your dreams and make the changes that you would like to make. There is no contract involved; it is simply an understanding that you have with yourself. If you think you would like to do something, start it, and find it isn't what you thought, accept that you gave it a try and recognize that sometimes that's good enough.

The point I want to make in this chapter is that you should begin to make yourself a priority. It is time to consider your wishes and dreams and not dismiss them. Move them from the back burner to the front one, so to speak.

We have all seen or heard about people who go back to college in their sixties and get their degrees. We have all seen or heard about people who have given up their lifestyles to travel the world donating time and money to the poor. Grandma Moses didn't start painting until she was 76 years old. I finally started my writing career in my sixth decade.

10. Make a list of the dreams you had or have for yourself. It doesn't matter what your age or gender is. It doesn't matter if your dreams seem impossible.

11. Now think about what prevented you from going after your dreams. Write down these reasons.

    Perhaps like me, you put your dreams and passions on hold while you helped someone else achieve theirs. And although you thought you might at some point go back to school or start a new career, you never seemed to do it.

12. Now make a list of the dreams you had that you actually accomplished. After you make this list, write down how you felt about your victories.

13. At this point, make a list of the people in your life who encouraged you to go for it.

14. Next, make a list of the people in your life who discouraged you from going after what you want.

    When I was 13 I confided in an aunt of mine that I wanted to be an actress. She was not the nicest person in the world. Her first response was, "Can you sing?" I said, "No." She then said, "Can you dance?" Again, the answer was "No." In my defense, I mentioned that Elizabeth Taylor and Natalie Wood also couldn't dance or sing. My aunt's response was that I didn't look like either of these actresses.

    To say I was shot down is an understatement. She would head up my list of the people who were a negative factor in my life. Even though I was able to get past her judgment and negative opinions when I was older, it took me a long time to get over the hurt feelings and emotional damage from what she had said.

This is a time to be honest with yourself. How much of what others have said to you has influenced your decisions in going or not going after your dreams?

15. When you look at your list of the people who supported you, did you list yourself? If you didn't, why didn't you? Isn't your own voice an important factor in your decision-making and in your life? And if not, why not?

    Here are some exercises to help you learn how to honor yourself and start to realize some of your dreams.

16. Make a list of the people whom you honor. For these exercises, if you are more comfortable using the word "respect" or "admire," please do so. These people can be famous or they can simply be the people in your life.

17. After you finish your list, look at each name and write down the qualities they have that you "admire."

18. Now make a list of the positive qualities you feel you share with these people.

19. Now list the positive qualities they have that you don't possess. Are these qualities ones you can work on? If so, think of ways you can do this. If you are stuck, perhaps talking with a close friend or relative can give you ideas.

20. It is time for you to create a list of the things you do to take care of yourself.

    If you find yourself staring at a blank piece of paper or blank screen for too long, then make a list of what you would like to do to take care of yourself. Use your imagination. For me, it would be a day at the spa.

It could even be a walk on the beach with a friend or my dogs. I can get lost in a good book while lounging on my hammock.

There are so many things we value in our society. We value our toys, our status, our children, and our sports teams. If someone were to ask you to name five things you value, would you have considered naming yourself? I believe most of us wouldn't. Think about why. Actually, let's change that. Think about why not.

Don't Make Decisions Based on Fear

I grew up in a household where my father worked and my mother stayed at home. We were by all means the average American family of the 1950s. I didn't know anyone from a divorced family. I didn't know anyone whose mother worked outside the home.

My husband and I divorced when our son was just two years old.

My mother told me that my girlfriends wouldn't want me in their lives, as they would think I was after their husbands (or vice versa). She told me that some families wouldn't want their kids to play with my son because he came from a broken family. Although this seems silly to me now, I believed her then. Again, the times were very different.

Life as a single mom was more of a challenge than I ever imagined. At 25 years old, I found myself living on my own, needing to find work, and looking for suitable daycare for my son. The seventies were very different than the present, especially where childcare was concerned. There weren't many choices, and the homes that "housed" little kids were unorganized and unlicensed. There weren't any restrictions on how many children caregivers could watch. Homes were not required to be childproofed. Caregivers smoked. Small apartments were used. And many places didn't have yards in which the children could play.

The thought of leaving my two-year-old son with a total stranger while I went to work was depressing and very sad for me. Cell phones weren't used then, nanny cams hadn't been invented, and background checks were unheard of. Every day when I left my son, he cried and begged me not to leave. Every day I felt as if I were a really bad mother.

There were days when I wanted to crawl under the covers and just cry, but I didn't have that luxury. I needed to make money and raise my son. There weren't any role models in my life. All of my friends were home with their children while their husbands went to work. None of my friends judged me or were critical, which didn't matter, as I was my own worst judge and was extremely critical of myself.

There wasn't any positive reading material about my situation. My son was referred to as a product of divorce or eventually a latchkey kid. To say I was frightened and unprepared would be putting it mildly.

My parents thought I should go back to my husband, and although on some levels it would have been easier for me, I knew it would be a mistake. Their philosophy was, "You made your bed, now lie in it." I was racked with guilt every time my former husband brought our son home after his visitation time was over. I felt that I was the reason he didn't get to see him more often. Although we both contributed to the breakdown of our marriage, I was the one who made the decision to leave. It was especially hard when Ryan cried at night because he wanted to see his daddy.

With each day came new challenges to be faced. I couldn't afford to allow my fears to stop me from making the decisions I knew needed to be made on a regular basis. I felt in the long run I was doing the right thing. But, at the end of the day, my fears were there and I would question my decisions on a regular basis.

I am sure there have been times in your life when you made decisions based on fear. Think about what these might have been. It could have been staying with an abusive partner because you feared being alone. It might have been staying at a job because you were afraid you wouldn't find another one. Some people feared taking a promotion because it meant they would be moving to a new area. Others feared joining a group because they worried that no one would like them.

For many people, patterns are familiar. It is what we are comfortable with. Take a look at your life now. Are you still making decisions based on fear? Are you stuck in a job that doesn't challenge you? Are you in a relationship where you are unsatisfied and unhappy? Do you feel you should "lie in your bed" just because you made a wrong decision years ago, or even as recently as yesterday?

1. How many times have you made decisions based on fear? What were your decisions? Write down your answers.

2. Now look at your list and write down what the consequences were of making decisions based on fear.

3. Next make a list of all the things you wanted to do but didn't because of your fears.

   Here are a few examples to consider. Did you want to go on a cruise with friends but had a fear of the ocean? Did you want to go on roller coasters but had a fear of heights?

   Perhaps you wanted to join a book club but feared you wouldn't have anything to offer. Going to the gym was a goal of yours, and yet you feared people would laugh at you. Or perhaps your shyness prevents you from having eye contact while talking to people. Your fears can be small or large; it doesn't matter. What matters is that you made a decision not to do something because you were fearful. What you didn't do was work through your fears.

   One of my first jobs involved knowing shorthand (an antiquated skill now, to be sure). This job would give me an opportunity to grow and make good money. Although I wanted to interview, I was fearful that I wouldn't be qualified. Instead of talking myself out of going to the interview, I decided to take a chance. I figured the worst thing that could happen is that I wouldn't get the job.

I knew if I didn't even try, I definitely wouldn't be hired. So I went to the library and checked out a book on shorthand. I spent the entire weekend memorizing as many symbols as I could.

I learned just enough and wrote my notes fast enough that I was able to draft the letter and type it during the interview. I got the job. One week later when I looked at my notes, I had to laugh, as I couldn't read any of them. I believe that in my desire to get the job, I actually memorized most of what my interviewer said to me.

This was a very important lesson to me. I could have easily rationalized why I would never be considered. Instead, I did what I could to eliminate my fear. And I was successful.

Some of the benefits of making decisions that are not based on fear are:

A. They help you to make positive changes in your life.

B. They enable you to try new things.

C. They allow you to make better choices.

In 1933, Franklin Roosevelt said, "The only thing we have to fear is fear itself." I find this very powerful. It is the fear that stops us, not the actual challenge.

4. Take the time now to think of and list ways in which you can overcome your fears. Practice the following lessons until they become second nature.

A. Recognize what your fears are.

B. Share your fears with someone you trust.

C. Think of ways in which you can push past your fears.

D. Practice making changes one step at a time.

5. Now think about the times in your life when you didn't allow your fears to stop you. For me, it was going to the job interview. For you, it could be something else.

6. Take the time to write down how you felt about working through your fears. Did you go to a party when you didn't know anyone? Did you volunteer for a job even though you didn't feel qualified? Did you join a sports team even though you aren't the best athlete?

   For me, it was pushing past my fears by moving out on my own, finding a job, making money, and making the best choices I could while raising my son. I was making decisions by myself for the first time.

   Whether you realize it or not, it is very empowering when you do something even though you are scared. When you realize that you are in fact capable, it gives you the confidence to face your next fear head-on!

Look for Your Blessings

I remember this day like it was yesterday. I was driving Ryan to preschool and was stopped at a red light. Ryan was in the back seat crying. I had an awful headache and was feeling so sorry for myself that I said out loud, "When am I finally going to get a break?" Right around this time, the light turned green. As I looked in the crosswalk, I saw a man pushing a wheelchair with a young boy in it. This child had both legs amputated.

In that very moment, I made a conscious decision to find at least one blessing each day. Whether it was looking at my healthy sleeping son at the end of the day or just knowing that we had food to eat and beds to sleep in, we were blessed. I decided that my family's good health and our having a safe place to live were the real blessings in my life.

It became important for my mental and emotional well-being to find a blessing every day. The fact that others had it "better" was not my focus anymore, as I was much more aware that many had it worse.

Are you the type of person who is always thinking that others have it better than you do? Does this take away from your own accomplishments? Do you sometimes feel as if you have a black cloud over your head? As hard as you try, do you feel you just can't seem to get ahead? The bills mount up. The weight won't come off. Your children aren't getting the grades that your friend's kids do.

When I was growing up, there was a common expression that went something like this: "Don't try to keep up with the Joneses." Try spending more time concentrating on what you have instead of what you don't have.

If you could truly appreciate how far you've come instead of how far you have to go, wouldn't that make you feel better? Instead, too many people gauge their own success by what someone else has. Look for and find your own blessings. Life isn't a contest or a race.

Why is finding your blessings so important? Does it really make a difference? YES!!! Perspective provides a wonderful view. It centers us and gives us real balance.

Instead of looking at what is lacking in your life, try to think about all that is good in your life. Appreciate the small things. Find a reason to smile. If you have two working legs and someone else doesn't, you have been blessed. It you wake up pain-free instead of in pain, you are blessed. Instead of using the number of flat-screen TVs as a measure of your blessings, try using your children's good health or having a roof over your head. See, you are already starting to feel better about your life. Aren't you?

If you are having a difficult time finding things to feel blessed about, try these exercises.

1. Make a commitment to find at least one blessing every day.

    Intentionally start looking for that one blessing throughout the day. As soon as you find one, even if it's small, write it in your journal. If you find more than one, list them all.

2. Throughout your day, think about the meanings of your blessings, and also write those in your journal.

3. If you are still having trouble finding your blessings, pay attention to the people you know who are less fortunate than you, and acknowledge what you have.

4. Any time life becomes difficult, review your list of blessings. Sometimes no matter how much we try to be thankful for what we have, life just gets the best of us. I would love to say that I was always able to see the bright side or have experiences that made me smile, but that wouldn't be true. There were many times when it didn't seem as if I had any blessings. I was frequently broke, always tired, and often second-guessing my decisions.

I went through times of being appreciative and then other times of feeling hopeless. When things became very challenging, I would take out a piece of paper and draw a line down the center. I would then list all the things that were negative in my life on one side and all the things that were positive in my life on the other side.

5. Take a few minutes to do the same thing. It doesn't matter if these are big things or little things. What matters is that they are important to you. Again, there are no right or wrong answers.

6. Now make a list of the things you have accomplished. They can be as simple as making a good dinner for your family or helping a friend who needs you. The idea is to find the positive aspects of your day, the things in your life that make you feel blessed, that make you smile.

7. Now make a list of the things that make you feel like your life isn't going well. What comes to mind? Is your job not as good as your brother's job? Is your home not as large as your best friend's? Be honest with yourself. The point of this exercise is to determine how much joy you get out of your life. If you are always comparing yourself with others, you will be on a treadmill that never ends.

Spend some time thinking about the things you have that others do not. Do you take family vacations? Do you have friends you can count on? Are there sports and hobbies that you enjoy? When people have parties, are you included? Don't make this just about material things; life is so much richer when people are more important than objects.

8. Make your list now of what you truly value, then look over it. Is it filled with experiences? Is it filled with people? Is it filled with toys?

9. Now write down how you feel about your priorities. Do you feel good? If you don't, spend some time thinking about the things you can add to your life that will give you pleasure. For some, it could be spending time with children. For others, it could be getting a pet or visiting a friend who isn't doing well. And for others, it could be taking a day to look over old photos and think of fond memories when you were in a good place.

Life is cyclic. When times are bad, we tend to think they will always be bad, and when times are good, that they will always be good.

My philosophy is that during the periods in my life when I am extra challenged and stressed, I try to pay extra attention to the positive things that matter, no matter how small.

Although my circumstances might seem dismal, it helps my overall disposition to grab hold of the good in my life. Although it seems trite to say, "If you think you are happy, you are," it has been proven that when you change your thoughts, you change how you feel.

Remember that what one person sees as a blessing, another one doesn't. We all have to figure out what we consider blessings. There is no formula.

Please don't see this as a two-week diet but as a daily project for life. Of all the things you can do for yourself, finding your blessings will truly change your perspective on life.

Don't Spend Time with Negative People

I was extremely happy after being hired for a job that I really wanted. I spent several months going to interviews, improving my résumé, and reading books about how to make a good impression.

I was overjoyed that I would be making good money, and the benefits package would cover medical, dental, and a retirement plan. I was going to be trained to work in a purchasing department as a buyer. There was room for advancement and I loved my working environment. Up until this point my jobs hadn't really provided any room for me to grow. Now I woke up every morning looking forward to being part of a team of very young and very creative people.

Because my commute was long and gas prices at that time were high, the company subsidized people who carpooled. So I added my name to the list on the bulletin board to try to find someone who lived near me so we could share the driving. I was very pleased that one of the women in my department was also looking to share a ride, so we worked out a schedule.

During the first week that we began our arrangement, this lady started talking to me about how unhappy she was at work. She didn't like her supervisor, the lunch breaks were too short, she didn't like the dress code, and she felt she wasn't appreciated. When she wasn't talking trash, she listened to unsettling talk radio. The various programs she listened to had talk show hosts who seemed angry all the time, and they were always trying to stir up the audience.

After a week of listening to her complaints about her job, I started to notice that she was affecting my mood. I now found myself getting anxious on Sunday nights and not wanting to go to work on Mondays. I also found I was becoming more and more impatient with everyone. Not just at work, but with my friends and also with my son. At the end of the ride home each day, I found myself upset and no longer pleased about my job.

I started to talk about this problem with a friend. She said, "Are you kidding, you love your job. What's going on?" After giving her details about what I was subjected to every day, my friend said, "Lose your car pool, turn off the negative talk radio shows, and start listening to music that you love." It was great advice then, as it is great advice now.

I was affected by this woman's drama and negativity, and so I did what was healthy for me. I removed the negative person from my life.

1. Who are the negative people in your life? Take some time to make your list. Whether they complain about their lives or they complain about other people they know, does their energy bring you down? No matter what seems to be happening in their lives, are they always seeing the downside of things?

2. Now list the ways in which these people are negative.

   Are they always finding something to complain about? Are they often in bad moods? Do they often talk negatively about people and about life in general? Do they spend their time obsessing about what other people have that they don't? Do they hang around negative people themselves or around negative environments?

3. Now take some time to think about what the impact is on you when you hang around the negative people in your life. Does your good mood change to a bad one? Are you less enthusiastic, less energized, and less

productive? Do you want to spend less time with the person or various people who are negative?

4. Conversely, take the time to think about the people in your life who are positive. Write down their names. They can be personal friends, family, or even famous people that you find inspiring because of their positive attitudes.

5. When you think about these people, do they usually seem to be in a good mood? Are they upbeat and do they smile easily? Do they inspire people rather than depress them? Are they people who spend time with other positive people in positive environments? Do they tend to respond to situations by looking at the bright side of things?

In the situation I now want to share, I was the positive person. When I was in my forties, a co-worker and I took a trip to New York. While we were in the same city, I was amazed at the differences in what we experienced. She saw filth and ugliness, and I saw a beautiful skyline. She saw too many people; I saw a vast, diverse culture. She saw the city as chaotic and frightening; I saw it as exciting and energizing. She chose to focus on the negative; I chose to focus on the positive. As we talked and shared our experiences, she started to look at things differently. She became more energetic and enthusiastic as we spent more time together.

My positive energy was contagious, and because of that, her trip became much more enjoyable.

It isn't always easy to make changes. It isn't always easy to close doors to friendships. However, if you find that no matter how much you are positive, the people in your life are always dragging you down, perhaps it is time to recognize their effect on you and remove these negative people from your life.

Take a look at your list of negative people. Decide who you need to and can remove from your life. You can do this by spending less time with them, or by severing your relationship entirely. Of course, you could first have a conversation with the person and let them know that although you would like a friendship (if you want one), you are finding it more and more difficult to be with them when they have such a negative effect on you. They might not even be aware of this. Or, perhaps it won't be the first time they have heard this, and hopefully they will take a look at themselves and make some changes. After all, we can't change what we don't acknowledge.

There will of course be people that we can't eliminate from our lives. Whether they are neighbors, family, or co-workers, it just isn't practical. In these cases try to limit the time you spend with them. Another thing you can do is to try to eliminate one-on-one time with them.

A great way to create a balance is by spending more time with people who are positive. Try spending some part of your day with upbeat, enthusiastic people. Try listening to programs about people who help others, people who spend less time talking about their own problems. Try to engage in activities that make you feel good. Exercising is great. Spending time with animals or young children or volunteering to help others might be good for you. Or it could be a hobby such as gardening, painting, knitting, or even getting lost in a good book. You have to figure out what helps you to feel good about your day, your life.

It is very important to listen to the dialogue in your head. Does it start out with "I can't," "I'm no good," or "Why me"? If so, turn your thoughts to "I can," "I am worthy," and "WHY NOT ME?"

As you meet new people, try to pay attention to how they make you feel when you are around them. Choose to bring more positive people into your life. Continue to remove negative people when possible.

6. Now think about yourself. Do you see yourself as a positive or a negative influence on someone else's life? How would your spouse, kids, friends, peers, and co-workers categorize you in this area?

Spend time evaluating yourself and how you affect others. If you are not sure, ask someone you feel comfortable with how they view you. After all, you don't want to be on the list of your friends who avoid you because they find you to be the negative force in their lives.

Learn to Face and Conquer Your Demons

Life is not a straight line. No matter who you are, where you live, or what you believe, life is filled with ups and downs. For many people, two steps forward and one step back is how life is. We often work through our problems, think we've solved them, and then believe we can just move on. When we least expect it, though, our past can come back to haunt us.

After years of being unsuccessful on my own, working through the sexual abuse I suffered as a child, I got a referral from my doctor to see a therapist. I decided it was time to commit to going through the process necessary to conquer one of my biggest demons: sexual abuse.

One of the first questions I asked the therapist was, "So, how long do you think it will take for me to feel better?" She looked me straight in the eye and said, "Your problems didn't happen overnight, therefore the solutions aren't going to happen overnight either." This made me think about the day I was in a bakery almost ten years earlier. A very large lady was looking at all the goodies she *wasn't* going to buy. She turned to me and said, "Wouldn't it be wonderful if I could lose my weight overnight … even though I know I didn't gain it that way?" We both laughed.

Therapy started out comfortably enough. I talked about my parents, I talked about my experiences, and I talked about my dreams and goals. I mentioned that I was getting more and more headaches and that my nights were filled with unsettling dreams. What I didn't do for a very long time was really get in touch with and talk about my childhood abuse. I never even connected that time with any of the problems I was having. In order to protect us, the mind sometimes buries unpleasant memories.

Although I had vague images of my childhood, for the most part I was a master at compartmentalizing what I didn't want to face. I had always downplayed what I went through. While I was recounting some stories of my childhood, my memories started to come back with a vengeance. Because I had done such a good job of suppressing what was disturbing, I spoke as if I were a third party, as if I wasn't the person who had lived my life. Talk about being detached from my own feelings.

After spending a few sessions with this therapist, she asked me, "How many more years do you want to go from one physical problem to another? Because, until you really work through this and face it, that is exactly what will happen. Aren't you tired of living your life like this?"

Really understanding and conquering this demon had been a lifelong struggle. And yes, I was tired of living my life without working through it. It really *is* easy to think, "We've talked about this, so there is no reason to talk about it again. We've cried about this, so there is no reason to cry over it again." Our lives aren't like chapters in a book. Everything we experience, all that we go through, is etched in our mind, body, and soul continuously.

My doctor used to say to me, "We are what we eat." I also feel we are what we think, we are what we do, and we are what we have experienced. Identifying our own personal demons, real or imagined, is the first step in learning how to conquer them.

1. When you think about any of your demons, what comes to mind? Take some time to think about your life. What are your monsters? Perhaps you were bullied as a child, or sexually molested as I was, or raped. Did you witness a horrible crime, or suffer a bad illness or accident? Did

you have a messy divorce, or did your parents have one? What haunts you today?

It was not my fault that I was molested as a child. It was, however, my responsibility and need as an adult to do everything I could to face and conquer this demon. Going through the process of therapy helped me to realize that many of my problems stemmed from being molested. My therapist encouraged me to find and talk with my abuser in order to give me the closure that I needed to move on with my life.

I spent many months thinking about contacting my abuser and how hard it would be for me to do that. I wrote letters about what I would say, and then I tore them up. I practiced saying things out loud. After almost a year in therapy, I made the decision to face him head-on. It took me many more months until I did just that. Since I knew he still lived in my old neighborhood, it wasn't difficult to contact him. I told him I wanted to talk with him, and he was willing to meet with me.

Although I was nervous about talking with him, I also felt confident that I would be okay. It was more important to me that I did this than anything he could say. It helped me to NOT feel like a victim.

I was fortunate that he sat quietly and listened to what I had to say. Afterwards, he looked me straight in the eye and said that all of my memories were accurate. He said that he was very sorry for what he put me through. He offered no excuses or defenses. I was fortunate that I could say what I had to, be heard, and close this door.

Obviously this isn't always the situation. The person could be dead, unavailable, or in denial. There are times when the circumstances are such that we have to find another way. That could be writing a letter. Or perhaps talking to a chair that we imagine the person is sitting in. There are many ways to release the anger, frustration, and fears that we have been living with.

2. Here are some exercises that might help you with the demons and monsters that still trouble you:

    A. Acknowledge on a daily basis the impact that your demons have on you, including fear.

    B. Contact a therapist and arrange for counseling.

    C. If desired, seek spiritual counseling.

    D. Talk things out with family and/or friends on a regular basis.

    E. Consider joining a group where people who have had similar experiences meet and talk about how they handle their demons. If there isn't one, consider starting one.

3. Spend time each day journaling your feelings until you feel less burdened.

I believe many of us feel as if we are the only ones that have the fears we do. I believe many of us feel that no one else would understand us if we talked about our personal demons. Instead of allowing your demons to get the best of you, wouldn't it be wonderful if you had someone to talk with who could give you the support you need?

If the people in your life confided in you what their monsters and demons were, would you judge them? Would you think there was something wrong with them? Or would you be open and supportive of them?

4. Make a list of the people you know who have battled with demons. Perhaps drugs or alcohol has been an issue. Perhaps holding a job or having the ability to be in healthy relationships has eluded them. If they came to you to talk about these things, what would you advise them?

5. Make a list of the things that you might suggest to them. Then look at your list and see which ones you could also benefit from.

6. Spend time each day working on your demons using your list of suggestions. Use your journal to track your success.

Facing your boogeyman, real or imagined, is the first step in giving yourself the emotional strength and self-confidence needed to finally come to terms with and eventually conquer your demons. I know for me, it did.

Learning to Forgive

I spent many years blaming my father for just about anything bad that happened in my life. I blamed him for my wanting to get out of the house; therefore, marrying way too young. Because of that, I blamed him when I quit college to help support my husband while he finished school. I blamed him for my poor self-esteem from all of the years he called me names and bullied me.

I blamed him because I was stubborn and defensive, which came directly from how I was raised. It didn't matter if he was at fault; it was just easier to blame him than for me to learn to take responsibility for my own actions and choices. It wasn't until I was in my forties that I was able to get perspective on my dad, on myself, and on my life. This helped me in learning to forgive him.

Because of the way I was raised and the decisions I have made, I am independent, quick-witted, and no matter what happens, I pick myself up and face each day head-on. My dad used to say, "You are who you are because of or despite your upbringing."

Although I don't recommend being raised as I was, despite all of my many challenges I continue to be a positive person who, as the saying goes (sic), "has been down, yet has never been out." I believe my dad would be very amused to find that I now quote him in a more positive way instead of a negative one. He would tell me, "Roni, you are going to spend much of your life working. Try to do something you are passionate about." Although he was a very successful businessman, he did not like what he did for a living.

He also used to say, "I grew up in Brooklyn in the thirties and forties; it was a very rough neighborhood." He would finish the story by saying, "There were as many doctors and lawyers that came out of the area as there were hoodlums and thieves." He was a firm believer that if you want something badly enough, you should find a way to get it. Although he never finished high school, he did finish the entire set of the *Encyclopedia Britannica*. He started with the A's, reading every page until he finished with the Z's. This took him many years, and he was very proud of himself for doing this.

My dad wasn't someone who quit easily, and neither am I. And for this I am grateful.

Really forgiving my dad took decades. I held on to hurts, I fostered disappointments, and I experienced great sadness that I couldn't have the kind of relationship with him that I desperately wanted.

I would love to tell you that I was able to forgive him before he passed away sixteen years ago; however, that wouldn't be true. It is, however, true that we reconnected in a much healthier way. Unfortunately it was when he was diagnosed with terminal lung cancer. We were able to talk and enjoy each other, even though true forgiveness for me didn't come until six or seven years after he died.

When you think about your relationships, do you tend to hold on to grudges, or are you the type of person who can easily forgive? Many people feel that until they can forgive, they can't really move on. I know this to be true.

1. Make a list of the people in your life that you can't seem to forgive.

2. After you do this, list the reasons why you cannot forgive them. Your reasons might be that you were bullied as a child, or you didn't get the promotion you felt you earned. Perhaps you were abandoned as a child,

or you feel your spouse and/or children take you for granted. Or are you the one who has a sense of entitlement? Or are there other things that make it seem impossible for you to forgive others or yourself?

I chose a beautiful day. A day similar to when my dad would go to the flying field and fly the airplanes he used to build. I was feeling guilty about having never gone to his gravesite, so I drove to the cemetery. It was my first visit since he died several years earlier. I walked over to his grave and sat beside it. I started by telling my dad about the family, about the great-grandson he never met, and how my mother was doing. Then I said, "Dad, are you proud of me now?" About this time I was into full-on tears. As I talked through my feelings, I found myself saying, "Dad, I forgive you." Although it was not the reason I went, I will never forget that day, because I walked away feeling cleansed and lighter.

3. Now think about how you feel about the people in your life that you can't forgive. Write down those feelings. For example, do you feel angry, frustrated, hurt, or disappointed toward these people? Or are you in fact angry, frustrated, or disappointed with yourself because you can't seem to forgive the people who have hurt you? This is very important. Forgiveness isn't always important for what it gives someone else; *it is a gift you give yourself.* It allows you to move on with your life in a more positive manner. The baggage that you are holding on to for the various things that were done to hurt you becomes your extra weight. Think about this. While your wounds are festering, does the person who you feel wronged you even know? Are they affected? Probably not.

4. Now make a list of the people in your life that you have been able to forgive. Write down the reasons you were able to do this. For instance,

were you able to talk through your particular issue with them? Did they show remorse for hurting you? Were you able to work through your anger in therapy, with a close friend, or just over time?

5. How did you feel when you were finally able to forgive?

6. Now think about the times and circumstances in your life when you were unable to forgive yourself. Write these down. Were you unavailable for your children when they needed you? Were you not attentive to an ailing parent? Did you cheat on an exam in class? Big or small, it isn't important. If it is stopping you from moving on, that is good enough.

Several years ago, I ended a long-term relationship. It was the right thing to do. However, it hurt someone I cared for very much. After many months of my not sleeping, not eating well, and dealing with bouts of crying and depression, I was given wonderful advice by a very dear friend. I had been staying with friends that I had known for over 40 years. I spent most of the day crying; I was a wreck. My friend's husband put his arms around me and said, "Roni, feel your guilt, acknowledge your actions, then forgive yourself and move on."

This was indeed a turning point for me.

7. Here are some exercises to help you learn to forgive.
   A. Choose one person each week from your list of people you said you could not forgive. Write down your reasons for not forgiving them.
   B. Now think about what it would take for you to forgive them. Perhaps an apology would help, or hearing them acknowledge that you have a point.

C. Now spend some time practicing what you would like to say to these people. After you feel comfortable, even though it may still be difficult, call or write that person and work through whatever problem caused you to not forgive them in the past. If the person is no longer alive, envision a scenario where you can have the conversation you would have liked. The worst thing you could do is to just blow this off and say, "Well, who really cares? I don't!" The simple act of forgiveness really does free the person who holds on to the grudge. This can't be undervalued.

It might seem as if forgiving oneself is easy. Not so. We are our own harshest judge.

8. Go back to your list of circumstances where you could not forgive yourself. List the problems or issues that remain unresolved. Each day pick a problem and write down what it would take for you to give yourself a break. If the situation can be resolved by taking a specific action—for example, returning money or merchandise that was taken—do it. If the problem can be solved by speaking with another person, do it. If the specific action is not possible, acknowledge that you made a mistake and promise yourself that you will try not to make a similar one in the future. Then say out loud, "I forgive myself." Use your name. Say it with conviction.

The outcome isn't always in our control when we ask forgiveness for things we have done to someone else. After all, they might not want to or be able to forgive us. It is possible the person you seek forgiveness from has passed away, or simply can't be found. But we can always forgive ourselves. Learning to forgive ourselves is key in learning to forgive others.

9. Take some time to think about the people who might be holding on to an old grudge or wound regarding something you did to them. Write down their names.

When I was in middle school, there was a girl in my class that I made fun of. She had very bad acne. Over the past many decades, I wanted to find her and tell her how very sorry I am for having teased her. The thought that I might have made her unhappy or cry really bothers me. I obviously cannot go back to that time and make things right. I don't even remember her name to look her up. While taking walks, I sometimes find myself thinking about her and imagining what I would say if we could talk. I start off by saying how sorry I am for the things I said. I let her share all her feelings. Then I simply say, "Can you forgive me?" In my imagination, she does. I do this because, although I can't get her forgiveness, it allows me to give myself a break by admitting that no one is perfect. I learned to be less critical and have made it a point not to comment or be judgmental when it comes to other people's appearance.

Whether forgiving someone else, yourself, or asking for forgiveness, the most important thing is to admit that you are human and to know that humans make mistakes. It is an important part of life. So is forgiveness.

Having Fun

After the breakup of my long-term relationship, I found myself becoming more isolated. I was not happy in my job. I was living with friends. My clothes were scattered around the room I stayed in, and most of my belongings were in storage. I had lost my independence and I felt as if I was being a burden to my friends, who never made me feel anything but welcome. I wasn't in a position to have my dogs very often, and I missed them horribly. And to top it all off, I wasn't certain what the future would hold for me.

It didn't matter that the decision to leave the relationship was mine; I was dealing with sadness and fear, and I was constantly second-guessing myself. My mind would not shut off at the end of the day and I found myself getting very little sleep. This caused me to lose focus during the day. I felt like an emotional wreck, and because I wasn't eating much or sleeping well, I ended up getting sick. What started out as a simple cold ended up becoming a bronchial infection.

My stress level was at a record high as I needed to find an apartment, hire movers, deal with packing, and eventually adjust to living on my own for the first time in my life. I went from living at my parents' home, to being married, to living with my son, and then eventually to sharing a home with my partner. I was very aware that I was starting over at a time in life when many people were enjoying the efforts of all the years of hard work and of raising a family. Many of the people in my circle were looking forward to finally having an easier, less stressful life. And although I was happy for them, this seemed to make it even harder for me to start over.

I had always been a person who managed to find fun, even during the most challenging times of childhood, and eventually, even though I struggled, as a single parent. I had always enjoyed sports, journaling, drawing, and playing board games with friends. Even when life seemed like a never-ending series of hardships, I had always made it a priority to be social and to keep up the activities that gave me pleasure.

Now it seemed as if I had lost the ability to enjoy myself and have fun. You could basically say that the percentage of fun at this time in my life was zero.

My friends began to worry about me and tried to encourage me to join them for movies, trips, parties, and/or dinners out. However, like many of us who get stuck in ruts or routines, I just couldn't get past my feelings of sadness and guilt. I truly lost the ability to enjoy pretty much any of the activities that I had previously been involved in. Although I didn't feel depressed in the sense that I couldn't function, I was most definitely functioning at a compromised level of energy.

I had always been a positive, upbeat person. That too changed. I now found myself becoming more negative. Negative in the sense that I couldn't see that things could get better. I wasn't able to make myself be or feel happy. Because of this, I certainly wasn't much fun to be around, and I knew it!

After almost a month I came to the realization that something had to change. And if things were going to change and eventually get better for me, I would ultimately have to be the person to figure it out. I needed to take stock of my life and take control of my life.

Part of my problem was that I wasn't sure how to turn things around; I didn't know what would help. I had always had the ability to bounce back, and now I couldn't. I thought about going back into therapy, or even joining a support group. I spent time walking around bookstores looking in the inspirational/motivational section. I never found anything that quite fit my needs.

One day while driving home from work I passed a park and I saw a group of people running. When I thought about the years that I spent running or walking, I remembered how much I loved it. There were times that I met friends after work to run, and there times when I would go by myself; it didn't matter.

Throughout the years, I could always count on my running to help me think more clearly and find balance in my life. Running as opposed to walking had always been my preference; however, I now made the decision that with a bad knee from a skiing accident years before, walking would be a much better choice.

And so my life started to change for the better when I again started taking long walks. It was how I started my day and it was how I ended my day. From this simple activity, I found myself becoming keenly aware of the dialogue in my head. I went from questioning my decisions and feeling sorry for myself to thinking about what I wanted out of life and what I wanted to accomplish. These very thoughts elevated my overall mood and eventually brought me new hope. I literally talked myself out of my funk. Shortly after this time, I made a decision to force myself to accept invitations, whether I felt like going or not. The more I went out, the better I felt. The more I laughed, the harder it was to be in a bad mood.

So many people live their lives with no time for real fun. They are too busy working, parenting, working and parenting, taking care of a sick loved one, or just being bogged down with responsibilities. In my case, I simply got stuck in my own situation and couldn't see the things that used to make me happy. I didn't bother to look at the upside of life, as I always had in the past. I failed to remember or acknowledge that in the long run, my decision to leave my relationship was in my best interest.

During my walks, I started to look more deeply into my decision to leave. I focused more on the reality that I was moving on from a relationship that no longer worked for either of us. When I had some perspective (time and space), I was finally able to acknowledge to myself that my partner and I had been arguing on a regular basis for quite a long time, and we were no longer treating each other in a loving or caring way. Admitting this truth to myself helped me to work through the anger and sadness I was feeling. In the end, I found myself feeling less stressed and more comfortable with my decision to move on. I was finally beginning to take control of my life.

1. In your journal or elsewhere, list the things that you enjoy doing by yourself. When you think of fun, what comes to mind? For me, this includes long walks, reading a good book, trying new recipes, etc. For you, it could be something else.

2. Now list how many of these things you actually do and how often you do them.

    Perhaps you are saying, "What free time?" Thinking of extra time is like thinking of extra money. There never seems to be enough.

    Do you find yourself so busy with chores or so tired from work and raising kids that you put your fun activities on hold?

3. Think about and then write down how you spend your free time. Are you balancing your checkbook, filing papers, catching up on laundry? While these things are necessary, you know they don't really belong on your "fun-time" list.

    I have a sister-in-law who has a stressful job, has raised two kids, and volunteers in her community. It amazes me how she finds the time to travel, hike, play golf, and entertain. Her philosophy is, "I have to work during the day, but I get to play on my time."

4. At this point, take out your calendar or look on your electronic device to study a typical week. First look at your workweek and then look at your weekends. Now, just as you would for a doctor's appointment or a meeting with a teacher at school, schedule "fun time" (*real* fun activities) on your calendar.

5. After you have scheduled fun time, pick one thing from your list of things you enjoy doing by yourself and insert that in the time slot you chose. It could be as simple as using your lunchtime to go to the park and read a book. Or perhaps right after work, stop at the mall and window-shop. Consider getting up a bit earlier on the weekend to garden or walk if that appeals to you.

6. Now take other items from your list and insert those on your calendar in the other times you chose. If you find that you keep putting off fun, picture a time when you engaged in fun activities and spend time thinking about how much better you felt.

    As time goes on, you will begin to find a comfort level in your percentage of responsibilities vs. your fun time. Give yourself permission to enjoy your life.

    There is a difference in having fun on your own and having fun with others. It is important to find time for both. Having fun by yourself allows you to reflect and gather your thoughts. Planning activities that you enjoy with others is healthy because you connect with other people. You don't isolate yourself from interacting and getting feedback.

7. Now, write in your journal the activities that you enjoy or enjoyed doing with others—friends, spouse, children, co-workers and/or neighbors.

   Again, think about your week. How much time in your week do you spend having fun with the people who are important to you? This doesn't need to be hours at a time. It could be incorporated into your day. If you work full-time, think about how you spend your time on your breaks and lunch hour.

   Try to find time in your day to enjoy an activity or interaction with other people, whether you choose to take walks with co-workers, start a book club at work, call a friend and chat about your weekend, go to the lunchroom and challenge another employee to a game of backgammon or cards, or whatever you do.

8. Make plans with friends to go to an art show, or go down to the beach and rent bikes. What do you like to do? What makes you laugh and smile? Think of this as a "playdate" for you. Remember to enter it in your calendar program or write it on your calendar *in pen* so that you give it the importance that it deserves.

   I have a friend who tends to say, "I escape my life one hour at a time." What she is saying is, "I make sure that even for short spurts I engage in the activities that bring me pleasure."

9. Make a list of what you think would be fun to do with your family, friends, and/or neighbors. I used mealtimes with my son to play word games. I also did this while driving him to school. Get creative. Have a block potluck dinner on the weekend. Plan a scavenger hunt with your children and their friends. Figure out what works best for you. Involve your children in these decisions.

I have friends who formed a group after their kids left home. They call themselves the Empty Nesters. There are around 20 couples. Once a month, a couple takes their turn at thinking of and planning a fun day for the group. No matter how busy their lives are, they always look forward to these group events.

I love to go to the park on weekends. I love seeing fathers flying kites with their young ones. Watching children riding their skateboards or bikes makes me smile, as I remember doing this when my son was younger. Even those of you that are not sports-minded can go to the park with your kids and dogs and toss a Frisbee. No cost, no fuss, yet lots of laughter and good times can happen.

Too many times I see the adults sitting on a bench watching. I wonder why more of them aren't in the sandbox with their kids or playing in the pool. Spending a few hours in the park could be play for you too, not just your kids. See it as play, NOT work.

About four years ago, a friend and I took our seven-year-old grand-sons to a water park. We joined the boys on all rides, carrying our tubes as well as theirs. We were the oldest people going down the slides. My friend observed all the children laughing on the rides while most of the parents and grandparents were sitting, watching, and waving with barely a smile on their faces. She said, "What a shame. Don't they realize how much fun this is?" And, even though it took some energy and we were tired, we laughed so much you couldn't tell who was having more fun— the boys or us.

Most of us are stressed out. Many of us are so tired at the end of the day or week that all we want to do is sleep or veg out. While it's import-ant to be rested, it is equally important to laugh and play. It doesn't matter how old you are.

There are so many ways to just relax and enjoy yourself. Your chores, your responsibilities, your worries will all still be there. Engaging in something that gives you pleasure will help you to be energized, which in turn will help you to handle your challenges better. The important thing is that the activities you choose give YOU pleasure.

10. Refer back to the list you made of the people in your life that you enjoy spending time with. Pick up the phone and call them and make a plan to meet and spend time doing something you both enjoy. Additionally, you can send an email or invite several friends to go for a spa day, or have a poker night. Don't just think about it or wait for someone else to plan something. At the beginning of each week, make it a priority to have several time slots on your calendar which include doing fun activities with someone else that gives you pleasure.

I called a friend last week and said, "If you have some time on the weekend, let's walk on the beach." She immediately said, "Yes." Simply smelling the ocean, walking barefoot on the sand, and watching the surfers was enough to get us through our chores and responsibilities. Other than gasoline, there was no expense.

There is an old expression that states, "All work and NO play makes Jack a dull boy." When kids are involved, play and laughter come with the territory. Try to get in touch with *your* inner child. This will give your life some balance when the bill collectors are knocking on the door and the laundry is piling up.

Whether you find moments in your day, hours on the weekends, or days off to travel, it is critical for your overall health and mental well-being to include fun in your life.

Learning to Trust Again

spent several weekends and evenings looking for a place to live. Once I found one that I liked, I hired a mover, enlisted the help of a few friends, and finally made the move from the comfort of my friend's home to my own place.

After I set up my new home and started getting into the routine of working, exercising, and spending time with my family and friends, life on my own was wonderful. I was finally able to have my dogs on a more regular basis as well as have space for my grandson to stay overnight when he visited. The condo I rented was in an area where it seemed as if everyone had a dog, and like me, enjoyed walking in the local parks. I was finally in a place I loved, and I felt very much at peace.

For the first time in a very long time, the decisions I made were totally my own. When I shopped, whether it was buying furniture or choosing dishes, towels, or even something as small as a waste paper basket, I felt like a kid who didn't have to compromise what I liked by checking it out with another person. At the beginning, it did seem odd. I was used to getting the input of someone else, and for the first time in many years I was taking control of my life. I loved it.

After about a year or so, I found myself thinking about dating. Although on some level I liked the idea of being in a relationship, I kept putting it off because I didn't want my cozy little nest to change. Getting up when I wanted to, eating when I felt like it, hanging in PJ's on the weekend if that appealed to me—ALL these things became a part of a lifestyle that I didn't want to give up. I was so comfortable with my life. I enjoyed my alone time and had fun trying new recipes, working on art projects, and cranking up the stereo, listening to the music I enjoyed.

I also loved spending time with my friends. I met them for a movie, dinner, or other activities that we had in common. I also walked my dogs, joined a local exercise class, and spent my free time at the pool at the complex where I lived, reading or swimming laps. I went from living with my parents and siblings, to living with my husband and my son, to eventually settling in with my long-term relationship. This would be the first time that I was living entirely on my own. It was a little bit of heaven. For those who ask, I would definitely recommend it. I learned more about myself during the few years I was on my own than I did in the previous 50.

As often happens, when we least expect it, something or someone is put in our path. I met someone I started to care about. The more time we spent together, the more we looked forward to being together and getting to know one another. Before we knew it, we felt a connection. After several months, we entered into a relationship.

It wasn't easy for me to let myself become vulnerable with someone again. We both brought our own baggage and pain from our past into the relationship. In the beginning, we walked on enough eggshells to make omelets for the entire neighborhood.

After experiencing hurts, broken promises, and uncertainties, it was very difficult for me to take down the walls and open up again. Over the years, I had become a master of shutting down my feelings. Rather than talking about how I felt, I pretty much kept everything bottled up inside. While I thought this was a great coping mechanism and the best way to get along, in reality it wasn't healthy emotionally or physically. It certainly wasn't healthy for any relationship I wanted to have.

I made a conscious decision early on that in my new relationship I was going to work on breaking unhealthy habits. I wanted to trust again, and I knew that I would have to be very aware of my responsibility in opening up. It wasn't fair for me to expect my partner to be a mind-reader. I believe many of us tend to do that in relationships, especially ones that we have been in for a long time. In the past, my thoughts were, "If you really loved me and if you really knew me, you would just know how I feel and what I need." I see now how unfair and unrealistic this is.

In my new relationship, we talked from the very beginning about the traps we both fell into in the past. We discussed our trigger points and we encouraged each other to base our relationship on healthy communication, honesty, and acceptance of each other. This is not always easy, especially when we are tired, frustrated, or angry at one another. We talked about listening to each other with an open mind and not jumping in before the other person finished talking. For me, this has always been a challenge, and still is. My mind starts racing, and before I know it I am in "defense mode." Some things are a work in progress. We all have things we need to pay attention to and improve on. For me, communication and trust are priorities in relationships of all types.

In our new relationship, we both agreed it was important that we didn't get caught up in the things that our old partners did to upset us. Along with this, we talked about how we each had contributed to the lack of communication in the past. We have both been aware from the beginning that it takes two people to create a safe and accepting environment, and more likely than not, it takes two people when things fall apart.

We are now three years into our relationship. We still continue to talk about our feelings, and we always strive to be supportive in a nonjudgmental way. Is this easy? Not always. Although it's an easy concept, the truth is that learning to trust again takes a lot of time, a lot of patience, a lot of love, and a lot of understanding.

Everyone has a different definition and different needs regarding learning to trust again. For me, learning to trust again means being vulnerable. What I mean by this is being comfortable with my insecurities, my tears, and my emotions. One of Dr. Phil's favorite quotes is, "Everyone needs a soft place to fall." At this point, I have that.

1. Think about the different people in your life with whom trust has been broken. In your journal or elsewhere, list these people. Remember as many people as you can. It could be your parents, siblings, teachers, or your extended family members. It might include one of your neighbors, your boss, or it could be a colleague, business partner, boyfriend, girlfriend, spouse, and/or your children. It doesn't matter what their relationship to you is.

2. Next to each name, write down what happened for the trust to be broken. Be specific. What did the other person do to you? Try not to be too petty here. Real trust is the subject, not small slights. Unless, of course, there have been so many incidents that you can no longer trust that person because of them. Perhaps you have lost trust where your feelings are concerned. They have hurt you once too often.

3. Now think about how you feel regarding the lack of trust. Are you angry, frustrated, hurt, or disappointed in others? Perhaps you are upset with yourself for placing trust in someone you shouldn't have.

Did you loan money to someone who didn't have the ability to pay you back, but you loaned the money anyway? Perhaps you counted on someone to help you move, and they didn't show up or even call to offer an explanation.

In your gut, you knew they didn't usually honor their commitments, and yet you chose to trust them anyway. At this time, write your feelings down.

4. Continue to think about yourself. Write down specific examples of times when you might have lost trust in your own judgment. Did you ask someone to watch your child even though they didn't seem responsible? Did you make a poor financial investment, one where you didn't do your homework and therefore put your family's financial security at risk? Did you ask a neighborhood kid to watch your house, even though you observed him or her hanging out with questionable friends? Perhaps you overlooked things because it was convenient or less expensive. All the red flags were there, and you chose to ignore them.

   Sincerely hold a mirror up to yourself where this is concerned. This is important, because learning to trust should start with your own judgment.

5. Now take this in a new direction. What would your friends and family say if you asked them if they thought you were trustworthy?

6. Do you believe they can count on you? Have you made promises and commitments that you didn't honor? Write down what these might be.

   If you are trustworthy and can be counted on, pat yourself on the back. Good job! But if you fall short in this area, whether that means not trusting your own judgment or having others unable to trust you, take the time to fix it. Think before you make promises and commitments. Don't volunteer if you truly aren't going to show up. Don't overextend yourself just because you want to seem like a good person at the time. When you give your word, it is very important that it can be counted on. If your words are NOT followed up with accountability, it won't take long for others to lose faith in you. Actions, as they say, speak louder than words.

7. Take some time now to think about the times when you reestablished trust with someone who had hurt you, or with someone you had hurt. Write down what happened. Did they reach out to you? Did you make the first move? Did you feel a sense of relief? Were you disappointed?

8. Think about how you felt after working through these trust issues. Were you truly able to move forward? Or were you hesitant to trust them until they changed their behavior and came through for you? Or are you always waiting for the other shoe to drop? Do you feel it is only a matter of time until you will be let down again? Take the time to write down your thoughts.

9. At this point, give much consideration to what it would take for you to trust your own judgment. Do you have someone in your circle that you can use as a sounding board? Are you part of a religious community where you can get counsel from your preacher or rabbi? Who are you close to that you can confide in and who can be objective? Write down the names of these people.

There are countless expressions regarding trust. The one I like the most is simply, "I have your back." What this means is that you don't need to look over your shoulder. "You can count on me to protect you." Trusting and feeling safe is important for all of us. While we shouldn't trust everyone who comes into our lives, trusting those close to us is essential to the overall relationship.

In an earlier chapter I addressed forgiveness and how important that is. Forgiveness is key in bridging the gap where trust has been broken or misused. Everyone deserves another chance. This doesn't mean that we blindly accept words alone. It is important to use all of our senses in determining who earns our trust and who doesn't.

10. I recommend the following exercises to help you learn to trust again.
    A. Look at your list of people whom you trust, people who have never let you down.
    B. Review the reasons you trust them. What qualities do they possess? Write that down in your journal or elsewhere.
    C. Now review your earlier list of people where trust was broken.
    D. Pick a person from that list that you would like to regain trust in.
    E. Contact that person and ask to get together with them.

    When you meet, talk with that person about the issue(s) that caused the loss of trust. Also share with that person your feelings about the event or events that occurred, and ask them to share their feelings with you. Talk with that person about what it will take to reestablish trust on your part. Then listen to what they would need, if anything. This is not meant to be confrontational. Honest communication is the key to success. Continue this process with anyone else on your list that you would like to regain trust with.

    When it comes to yourself, start by not overcommitting to things you can't deliver on. Think before you make promises. Use words like "I intend to" or "I would like to." When you tell someone that they can count on you, be certain that they actually can.

    Learning to trust is a process for some. Try to be fair. Try to put yourself in someone else's shoes. Compassion, communication, and patience are all vital to reestablishing bonds that have been broken.

Love and Happiness

Life was good. I was working as a field sales representative in the electronics industry. Most of my career was spent either working as a procurement agent buying electronics or working for a distributor selling electronics. I was good at what I did, and I was well respected. The problem was that the various positions I held never really challenged me, nor did they give me any true personal satisfaction. I was, however, appreciative that my job paid the bills and that most of my customers were professional and easy to work with.

One of the many perks of my field sales job was that I had the freedom to plan my days. I have always been an outside person, and I had felt cooped up working in an office. It is one of the main reasons I left purchasing. As a purchasing agent, my days were spent in a cubicle sitting in front of either a computer or a salesperson.

Being in the field allowed me to spend several hours each day traveling. For many people, this wouldn't be a good fit. One of the main reasons is the lack of structure and so much time spent in and out of a car. But it was perfect for my personality. I hated office politics and small cubicles. Having what we refer to in sales as "windshield time," because the car is our office, gave me a sense of freedom that I loved.

My normal work routine was to get up in the morning and set up appointments to visit my customers. I did this from my home office either by making phone calls or by sending emails to various purchasing personnel or design engineers. I would then get in the car and drive to my appointment to make these account calls. My job also included attending trainings on the various products we sold and meeting with support personnel to plan strategies. I greatly enjoyed this part of my job. Negotiating contracts, discussing methods to improve upon a system, and sharing ideas with others was invigorating and fun for me. Overall, I enjoyed a successful career; however, I never loved what I did and my choice in careers never made me happy. I always envied people who had a passion for their jobs. We spend so much time working. Finding a vocation that combines our passions and interests and allows us a satisfying financial lifestyle is the best of both worlds.

Because I never found work particularly satisfying, I filled my nights and weekends with the activities that I loved. Sports have always been high on the list of ways I like to spend my time. Over the years, I played tennis, swam, and was an avid bike rider. I skied, ran in 10K runs, and was comfortable with a racket, paddle, or ball in my hand. Growing up with two brothers and a father who loved sports, I found that keeping up was a way of acceptance. In my youth, I was called a tomboy. Organized sports for girls wasn't ever an option until I was in my late teens. One of my oldest friends, who continues to share my love of tennis and team sports, is always saying that we were born one generation too soon.

At present, long walks with my dogs, hikes in the local hills, and occasional laps in a pool keep me moving and in shape.

I have also always been a daydreamer. I was the kid who sat in the classroom looking out the window at the sky while the teacher talked.

My job allowed me the luxury of rolling down the windows in the car and opening the sunroof. I love the feel of the wind or warmth on my skin. When I would think about looking for another line of work, I always justified staying because having the sunroof open and my stereo blasting was so important to me. It filled my soul.

I could stare at clouds for hours, finding animals in them. I always preferred long walks outside to a treadmill in a gym. I could get lost in my thoughts on a walk or lying in my hammock. My favorite place has always been the beach. While it has always been challenging for me to fully relax, the waves, warm sand, and the smell of the salty ocean give me the inner peace that I believe all of us need. This I can trace to my childhood.

Every year from the time I was 12 until I was 18, when school ended for the summer I went to Brooklyn to spend three months with my relatives. These trips were the best time of my life. Unlike the Pacific Ocean, the Atlantic Ocean was warm and inviting. My relatives lived very close to Brighton Beach and Coney Island. Because I was able to escape my troubled childhood for several months every year, I felt safe, loved, and secure. The ocean is simply a reminder of that time. It's interesting how our early childhood experiences can stay with us for our entire life.

My job paid the bills, and I engaged in the activities and hobbies I loved. My long-term relationship was declining at this time. There were many reasons for this. The main one was simply that we were drifting apart and I was not satisfied with a relationship that lacked good communication and closeness. Although at the time I wasn't planning on leaving, the two of us were clearly not enjoying each other, and we started to spend more and more time with other people.

My health was good, as was the health of most of my family and friends. There were the normal challenges life brings, but other than that, life seemed good. And yet, there was still something missing.

I considered midlife crisis. I thought about the eternal question of, "Is that all there is?" And the one that many ask, "Why are we even here?" For me, it felt like a combination of all these things. With more questions than answers, I decided to indulge myself and spend time seeking some answers that would either satisfy my curiosity or at the very least amuse me for a while.

So I started to do what I have always done when trying to understand what was going on with me: I spent time by myself with my thoughts. I took long walks and allowed my mind and imagination to wander. I then went through a ritual of making a mental list of my blessings, and followed this by making a mental list of what didn't satisfy or work for me. After many weeks of doing just this, it dawned on me that I lacked something to feel passionate about. For me, love and happiness did not come in the package of another person. For many it does. For me it came from being passionate about how I spent my time. We all have a different definition of love and happiness.

Although I hadn't always known *what* was missing, I always knew that I had yet to find it. So I began to indulge myself in spending time trying to figure out what was lacking in my life, what would truly give me pure love and happiness.

I started by spending my free time going to bookstores and wandering around the inspirational or motivational section. While walking or driving, I would spend many hours listening to music—songs that didn't just get me thinking, but that also lifted my spirits and filled my soul with excitement and hope.

I also bought a journal and started to write down my thoughts and feelings, which eventually turned into my writing blogs. I wasn't sure what would come of what I considered a journey of discovery. I just accepted that at this point in my life, it was important for me to really *feel* what was going on and to try not to overthink things. Not an easy thing for me to do. In all honesty, a VERY difficult thing for me to do.

I have always considered myself a spiritual person, and although I am not particularly religious, I do believe in a higher power. I tend to spend many of my walks appreciating all that nature offers us. I am often overwhelmed and amazed at the beauty all around us. I can stop to watch a bird for what seems like hours, or look at flowers and surrounding trees and just be in awe of the colors. I spend much of my thinking time wondering about the miracles that we take for granted.

So it wasn't a large leap when I found myself enrolling in a meditation class. It was a six-week course, the first one I had taken. As I sat in class breathing deeply, listening to our guide help us relax, my mind and heart started to open up and I started to experience the calm and inner peace that had eluded me.

Along with guiding us through opening up our chakras, a kind and wonderful woman named Alina blessed us with much wisdom. Each week, Alina started our class with a ten-minute talk regarding various aspects of life. The point of these talks was for her to help us look at life with a different viewpoint and perspective, one that might help us to understand ourselves, our actions, and the world we live in.

Halfway through the series of classes, Alina asked a question of us. She said, "Give me your definition of love and happiness." One by one we shared our list. They consisted of things like "Meeting the love of my life; spending time doing the things I enjoy, like traveling, reading, and sports, etc." A few people mentioned being with their pets, spending time watching grandkids, and/or joining friends for movies and dinner. And on the list went.

My personal list consisted of being comfortable with myself, making decisions that I felt good about. Of course, my family, friends, and pets were high on the list of things that gave me pleasure; however, it was equally important to me that I always strove to be a positive influence and not harbor negative thoughts.

One of the points Alina was trying to make was that finding love and happiness was a key to rooting out depression, anxiety, listlessness, and so on. In order to really achieve love and happiness, we needed to start with learning to love ourselves. She said, "Not when you lose five pounds, not when you finish your degree, not when you achieve financial success." She went on to say that these things might add to our lives; however, if we didn't love ourselves, we would in fact just keep looking for other goals and trophies, thinking that once we achieved them we would be happy.

It became very clear to me that love and happiness are integral parts of our lives. And it starts with how much we value who we are. When I find myself forgetting this, I spend some alone time and reflect on this lesson to refocus my energies.

1. In your journal or elsewhere, write your definition of love and happiness.

2. Now, write down the names of the people in your life that you love who bring love and happiness into your life. This shouldn't just be a romantic love or a love for a family member. Think of friends, neighbors, and even co-workers who bring a smile to your face.
    A. Does it make you feel happy just knowing you will spend some time with them?
    B. Is it the activity that you engage in, or like me, is it more important that there is laughter and closeness that you feel? (If I didn't mention it before, laughter, fun, and connections with others are extremely high on the list of what I value most.)

3. Now it is time to make a plan to spend some time with these people. The ones that make you smile. The people who elevate you. Whether it is for coffee, breakfast, or just a walk at the beginning or end of your day, start to include these people in your life more often. It doesn't matter what

you do, whether you get together with neighbors to have a block party or you organize a book club with friends who enjoy reading.

Whether your friends are single or come as a couple, you can arrange to get together for a BBQ or card game or whatever comes to mind. Fathers and sons and mothers and daughters can arrange special days together. Or, of course, fathers and daughters and mothers and sons should find the time and activities that they can enjoy with each other.

Every time I log onto Facebook, I see someone posting a quote about the friends who are there for them through thick and thin, or various quotes regarding removing negative energy from your life. Although these quotes and words of wisdom are posted and reposted, I wonder how many people really practice them. Words are easily thrown around. Truly living a life that incorporates them into our everyday dealings with people takes awareness, patience, and practice.

Use your imagination. The important thing is to increase your level of love and happiness. This starts with making a conscious effort to make a plan, because if you don't, I guarantee it won't happen.

Ask yourself, "Does my level of happiness rise when I am at the park listening to children playing, or when I get as far as possible from noisy kids?" Perhaps a warm bubble bath and some alone time is what you need, or do you prefer a crowded mall with all the stores calling your name? I immediately get happy when I see a dog. They have a special place in my heart.

What you want to achieve is to identify what works for you. This is, after all, your journey. This isn't about what others like. This isn't about what you think you should be doing. My feeling is that if I am the one taking the journey, I want my shoes to be as comfortable as possible. Think about this, and write down some of your thoughts on this subject.

4. Now spend some time and think about the activities that you love, ones that lift your spirit and bring you joy. Write these down.

   My mood always rises when I lie down on my hammock with a book, or indulge in the simple act of daydreaming. Whenever I ride up or down the coast, I immediately feel a sense of joy. For you, it could be gardening, listening to music, or playing an instrument. Again, these should be things that make you happy. There are no right or wrong answers. And you don't have to stick with a plan just because you made one. If you try something and you don't like it, try something else.

5. Now take some time and make your own list. Try to come up with approximately ten activities that you love and that bring you happiness.

6. Look over your list. Write down the activities that you aren't engaging in.

7. Jot down the reasons you aren't including these in your lifestyle. Are they activities that you don't feel you have time for? Or do you find you want to do things that are out of your price range? Perhaps you want to do needlepoint or paint but you are concerned that you don't have the aptitude. You would love to take a cooking class but feel that you can't afford it.

   After you study your list, think about what you can do to achieve some of it. If you want to learn to cook and a cooking class is too costly, perhaps you can gather several friends who are good cooks. Have each one bring a recipe with the intention of teaching the others how to cook this item. Or if you'd like to learn to do needlepoint and there aren't any classes nearby, try finding a group of women in your community who would also like to do this. Invite them over, along with people who have experience. Sitting around a table sharing ideas and talents is an excellent way to learn something new while meeting new friends. There are so many ways to get the same results. Be creative. This will add to your overall happiness.

8. Now study your list. Break it down. Find something that you are willing to try, even if it is out of your comfort zone. Come up with your personal plan.

   A few years ago, a friend of mine talked me into taking an afternoon painting class with a local artist. Although I had indulged in sketching, working with acrylics was new and very scary to me. Most of my sketches were of cartoon characters. We were going to paint a red rose. I felt totally out of my element and was certain I would make a fool of myself. Although my initial response was, "No, I am going to pass," I decided that the worst that would happen is that my rose wouldn't be very good, and would that really be such a big deal?

   So I signed up for the class and with much skepticism joined eight other women for what turned into a wonderful day.

   Although artist Georgia O'Keeffe, famous for her paintings of flowers, has nothing to worry about, I did a fine job and felt good that I at least tried something new.

   Again, you don't need to make a long-term commitment to a hobby or activity; even a few classes could give you an indication if it is something that will bring joy into your life. Even if things don't work out, you might make a new friend. Or just have an experience and a story to tell the family at dinnertime, as I did with my rendition of a rose.

9. Besides planning fun activities for yourself, your friends, and your family, I highly recommend planning at least one selfless activity every month

that would give someone else love and happiness. If you are having trouble coming up with one, try volunteering at an animal shelter, or assisting an elderly person in the neighborhood by taking them for an outing or cooking a meal for them. Offer to help a single parent who could use a break from her children or chores. Or better yet, come up with your own list of something to do. Start that list now. These can be short-term or long-term goals. This is not a commitment; it is a start to giving real consideration to giving back. It truly is amazing how good this can feel.

My niece and nephew spent several spring breaks in college working for Habitat for Humanity. Love and happiness shouldn't just come from doing things for you. The expression that "It is better to give than receive" is so true.

Remember that love and happiness can and should be a balance of nurturing and taking care of you along with extending yourself to help others.

Think about how much more worthwhile your life would be if you knew that the world was a better place simply by you being in it.

Most of us have to work. Many of us take care of our family and do the chores that come with living. So many times, we forget that life can and should be fun. Give yourself permission to be happy. It is your right!

Where Do You Get Your Inspiration?

I have always envied those who felt inspired—inspired in general, inspired to create something, or inspired to help themselves and others. This was an area that was missing from my life.

Although I didn't love my jobs, there were aspects of them that I enjoyed. I engaged in activities that were fun. I joined organizations that were meaningful. I traveled many parts of the world. I am for the most part a happy, upbeat person. And yet, I can truly say that inspiration eluded me. I suppose since my life was basically good, one could think, "So what?" But I felt as if a *little* something was indeed missing.

So I made it a priority to really search for things that not only made me happy and that I loved, but that truly gave me inspiration. There is a difference. Perhaps a subtle difference, but it is there. Happiness and love fill the heart, whereas inspiration fills the soul. Perhaps this is a personal opinion; however, it is how I view it.

During this time, a friend of mine suggested that I take a sketching class. Not a one-day class, but a series of classes. Both my mother and a favorite uncle were talented artists. From the time I was little, I loved to doodle and sketch. I had never shared anything I'd drawn; however, I took a chance and showed a friend some of my work. My friend looked at many of my drawings and thought they were really good. Me? I could not see what she saw. I would imagine this came from a critical, perfectionist father and an older brother who excelled in everything he tried.

I think that if we could only see ourselves as others do (as my friend saw me, for instance), we might not be so hard on ourselves.

Even though I felt my artwork lacked any real talent, I decided to see what was available. After all, I enjoyed drawing, and as I said earlier, I was on a path to explore parts of me that would ultimately give my life meaning and inspiration. I was open to any and all suggestions that made sense time- and money-wise. The interesting thing about opening ourselves to new adventures is that we tend to look at the world differently. Travel also does this. It takes us out of our comfortable world and forces us to expand our mind by expanding our experiences.

I found a six-week sketching class at a local college and signed up. I bought all the materials required and joined eight other students in a two-hour class once a week. I was immediately given positive feedback on my drawings from our instructor, and to my surprise, I even started to have a more positive view of my work. I recognized the importance of encouraging creativity, as opposed to judging it, regardless of one's age.

As in so many things, there is no right or wrong way. Creative expression is as individual as clouds in the sky. As children, my generation was taught to color inside the lines. We now allow and praise young people to think out of the box and do what comes naturally to them. There are many famous artists, past and present, who never adhered to this philosophy of staying within the lines, Picasso being an obvious example.

It amazed me how this simple act of sketching opened up my mind and my spirit to everything around me. I found myself looking at the skies differently. I noticed that colors were more intense than they had been. Although I had always enjoyed observing the mountains and beaches on my walks, it was now kicked up a notch as I looked even more closely, as an artist might.

On my walks, I relied less on my iPod to entertain me and more on my eyes and ears. I paid keen attention to all the beauty that surrounded me and found I wasn't just seeing the sights; I was actually experiencing them. The difference is that I didn't take them for granted. I was amazed and in awe of them.

As time went on, I started *thinking* in terms of inspiration. Because my mind-set was changing, so were all my senses. Music had become more meaningful, and sunsets were more intense. Instead of reading articles about the world's problems, I looked for reading material about people who performed heroic and unselfish acts.

It seemed that the more I did this, the more I found that inspiration was all around me. I read about people who fostered animals, volunteered in the inner cities, and formed groups to feed those less fortunate. I read stories about young people who donated part or all of their birthday money to children who didn't get gifts. Young people that started clubs at school to send blankets and socks to soldiers. Or those who collected crayons and paper to send to kids who lost their homes and all their belongings in floods or disaster areas.

I started becoming inspired by family members and friends. It was as small as helping a neighbor move, or as large as my sister-in-law who gave up vacation time to help a breast cancer patient.

Many of us go through our lives living without inspiration. We get up. We get ourselves going, and in many cases, get our families going as well. Maybe we go to work all day, and then we socialize with friends or co-workers after work. Or maybe we stay home and take care of children and perform household duties. Maybe we shop, cook, make dinner, do the laundry, help with homework, watch TV, and then crawl into bed just to get up the next morning and start the process all over again. This is, after all, the routine of living life.

Without inspiration, life can lose its zest and excitement, which translates to feeling low energy or being tired, sad, depressed, etc.

Inspiration is different for each of us. Some of us get inspiration from music, art, movies, theater, books, dance, and so on. For others, it comes from a hobby like drawing or painting, sewing, gardening, or writing. For yet others, it's a spiritual experience one gets from going to church, synagogue, a mosque, meditation center, yoga, and/or from prayer. Some get inspiration from listening to great speakers or participating in a cause that is bigger than themselves. Everyone truly is unique in how they experience inspiration. One thing is for sure—inspiration is all around us; we just need to open our hearts and minds to find it for ourselves.

1. Take out your journal and think about the things that inspire you. Make a list of what these are.

2. Now spend some time and think about how much time during your week you actually spend engaging in these activities. Write that number down.

    I believe balance is essential to our overall well-being, whether we are talking about food, work, playtime, or sleep and relaxation. When you give thought to your days, weeks, months, and years, can you honestly say that you engage in enough activities that truly inspire you? Or are you "sleepwalking" through your life?

    Isn't it about time for you to make inspiration an integral part of your life?

3. Take out your calendar and randomly find spaces to simply write or type the word "inspiration." Do this for several days every week. This exercise is to help you remember to think about looking for things that inspire you.

    Most of us don't need to put our daily tasks on our calendar. We have our routines: Whether you brush your teeth first and then wash your face. Whether you have a cup of coffee and then get dressed. Or whether you work out in the morning or later in the day, you incorporate habits, chores, and activities into your life.

If finding inspiring things is new for you, seeing the word on your calendar will remind you to call a friend who needs help, donate your time to a charity, or go to your playlist and listen to certain songs.

4. I would now like you to think about the people in your life: friends, family, neighbors, or those you come in contact with. Make a list of the ones that inspire you.

    A. Do they donate time?

    B. Are they more evolved when it comes to spirituality?

5. After you list their names, write down why they inspire you. It could be as simple as their getting out of a bad relationship, even if life is harder for them in the short term. It could be because they lost a child and started a fund for others who have experienced the same tragedy. Do they advertise on Facebook to help find dogs a foster or adoptive home?

6. When you think of these people, what comes to mind? Do you smile? Do you wish you could find a cause that you can support? If the answer is yes, think about what that might be. Jot down your answers. Perhaps you can talk with people or do your own research to find what inspires you.

Now think about famous people that you find inspirational. For me, it is Bill and Melinda Gates. Not because of the money they donate, but because they actually get involved on a personal level. It would be easy for them to simply write a check. They also give time to researching and creating schools and infrastructures for underdeveloped countries. Not everyone has the ability to do this. However, we all have things we can and should be doing.

7. Next, hold up a mirror and do some self-reflecting. Do you see yourself as an inspirational person? If you were to ask the people in your life if they found you an inspiration, what do you think they would say? Write down your response.

We all have something to offer. For some, it's on a stage or pulpit, and for others it's in the community or neighborhood. Step out of your comfort zone and take on at least one activity that gives back to society in a way that inspires you and others.

It could be volunteering at a homeless shelter or fostering an animal. Or maybe it is helping troubled teens or battered women. If you are healthy, have family, and a support system, you are fortunate. Many don't. Take the time now to jot down the various activities that come to mind.

A life that takes and doesn't give back lacks a compassion that is essential to the world we live in. Most who give unselfishly find that they receive much more than they give.

I cannot emphasize how very important and powerful inspiration is to your life.

When your days are coming to an end, do you want to look back over your life and wish you had done more to help others? Don't live a life of regrets. You can and should take control of who you are, what you do, and more importantly, what you give.

Final Thoughts

Life is a gift. It is fragile and it is short. Take the time to know yourself. We spend much of our early life in school learning to read, conquer math, and study history.

We then learn a job, how to maintain our car, operate our electronic devices, and various other tasks required to get along in our world.

How much time do you take to get to know yourself? To understand how you tick? Along with knowing yourself, how much time do you take to understand others and to learn how they tick? Perhaps if you make it an integral part of your life to do this, you will learn from both your successes and your failures. You will become more aware and understand why you repeat your mistakes and don't take responsibility for some of your choices.

Perhaps if you take the time to really get to know yourself and the world in which you live, your life will be more fulfilling and will give you the happiness and peace that you truly want and deserve to have.

Something to think about, don't you agree?

Acknowledgments

Anyone who has written acknowledgments on their book will understand how easy, yet how hard, this part is. It's easy because thanking people for their support, encouragement, and love is a pleasure. It's hard because I don't want to forget anyone or shortchange anyone with my appreciation, as I feel so blessed to be surrounded by such great friends and a family that I love with all my heart.

It started with my friend Susan Sherman, who said over coffee one day, "You have a way of getting to the heart of a problem. I believe you have a book in you, and I have a friend who is a publicist." Your faith in me has given me the confidence to finish what I started four years ago. Lindi Stoler and I worked together to take my life and use it as a springboard to help guide my readers as they navigate their own lives. Nancy Arkin was one of the first to read my poems and short stores. Her response was, "I don't know what anyone else thinks, but I like the way you write." You helped me to go deeper, and your patience and encouragement was constant, and I thank you.

My son Ryan has made me proud from the moment he was placed in my arms. You make being a mother an easy job, as you are a sweet, loving, and supportive son. My daughter-in-law Julie inspires me daily with her strength, goodness, and love. My grandson Travis has my heart. He's not only handsome, smart, and a great basketball player, but also a kind soul who makes this world a better place.

I want to thank Harvey Kugler for being my son's father. Judy Perlman, I learned so many valuable lessons from you. Opening my heart and my mind are just two.

If I could have had a sister, it would have been my brother's wife Nancy. You are one of my best friends, and your unquestioning love and support is a constant in my life. I have two of the best brothers a girl could have. They are always there when I need them. They are kind, supportive, and two of my very favorite people in the world. They also keep me real with their brotherly jabs and inside jokes. I want to thank my mother for believing I was beautiful even when I looked my worst. She always told me I could accomplish anything I set my mind to.

In no particular order I have to mention these friends: Shelley Wolfe, Debbi Turner, Susan Pickup, Lauren Zemechman, Bonnie Gottlieb, Maggie Stone, Kathy Gotch, Eileen Robin, Kat Figel, Robin Horowitz, Bub Pickup, Susan Cotton, Larry Cotton, Steve Weiner, Jeff Brown, Gail Lynn, Kelly Murphy, Marjie Brown, Marti Moray, Violet Bohjalian, my pickle ball and my mah-jongg friends.

Shelley is always in my corner and is one of those friends who would take a bullet for me. While encouraging me to live my passion, she protects me by keeping me grounded. Debbi, who has been in my life since we were kids. Although we are as different as night and day, you have been one of my best and closest friends through thick and thin. Your loyalty and sense of fairness is always present. Susan P., I am honored to be your friend. You walk the walk. While asking for very little, you are one of the most loving and giving people I know. Bub, one of the best men I know, I feel so fortunate to have you in my corner. Bonnie, from the very beginning you have found my blogs and writings to be inspirational, and your encouragement has and is what helps me when I feel like giving up. Lauren, who I knew as a casual acquaintance, became a cherished friend. I trust your judgment and count on your viewpoint. I thank you for filling in the void during the critical time in the publishing of my book. Kat, another friend who believed in me from the very beginning, and is always cheering me on. Maggie Stone, a partner in crime. Again, one of the first people to encourage me to go for my dreams. We have shared many adventures, and I cherish our friendship. Sue and Larry Cotton, you are both fans of my writing, and your love and support means so much to me. And this is why this is so hard. I could simply go on and on when it comes to the blessings I have regarding the support and love in my life.

Goldenbear, Linda Schwartz, Kim K, Alina Shalev, Kristy Roberts, and Bethany Kelly have all been very important guides for me. I do believe the universe has a way of putting people in your life when you need them most. It is so important to acknowledge this. No one goes through life alone. Whether you believe in angels or an afterlife, or you believe this is a one-shot deal, remember to be thankful for those people who hold your hand, hug you when you need it, and help you to learn the lessons that will guide you.

Bethany, before you and I started working together, I was hesitant about the process of self-publishing. You assured me you would be there to make this a positive experience. And, that you did! I value and trust your instincts. Thank you!

Dan Neira, the best shoulder, marketer, and media guy in the world. He has been a voice of reason and has made me look good in all my videos. You are amazing!

Frank Steele, your words of encouragement are so appreciated. You made the editing process easier than I could have imagined.

Chellie Campbell, a respected writer and motivator. When you read my proposal and said, "Girl, you sure can write," I cannot express how much this has meant to me.

Grandma Helen, you gave me unconditional love, which is the reason I have the capacity to love my family without question. You were the single most important person in my life, and I miss you every day.

If you are fortunate enough to have a passion, go for it. Don't let anyone tell you that you are NOT good enough. This is your life—live it your way!

About the Author

Roni Kugler has tens of thousands of online followers for her popular motivational, inspirational blogs. She has a strong following on YouTube, with over 36 videos in which she talks about everyday challenges.

Roni has written an interactive manual available on the web: 5 Ways To Avoid Losing A Loved One Due To A Senseless Fight.

12 Ways to Discover What Makes You Tick is her first book. She is currently working on her second book, which addresses other challenges that many people face.

Roni lives in Southern California, where she enjoys an active life, including tennis, hiking with her dogs, and spending time with family and friends

Using solid examples from her own experiences, Roni employs humor to guide readers on their journey to become their best self. Roni has a way of taking life issues that seem complicated and reducing them to manageable steps. Her nonjudgmental approach and friendly attitude invite readers to come for advice, but stay to enjoy a cup of coffee.

http://ronikugler.com/
https://twitter.com/RoniKugler
https://www.pinterest.com/ironik1
https://www.facebook.com/roni.kugler

Made in the USA
San Bernardino, CA
13 September 2016